Early Babylonian Letters from Larsa

Ancient Texts and Translations

Series Editor
K. C. Hanson

Robert William Rogers
Cuneiform Parallels to the Old Testament

D. Winton Thomas, editor
Documents from Old Testament Times

Henry Frederick Lutz
Early Babylonian Letters from Larsa

Albert T. Clay
Babylonian Epics, Hymns, Omens, and Other Texts

Daniel David Luckenbill
The Annals of Sennacherib

A. E. Cowley
Aramaic Papyri of the Fifth Century B.C.

G. R. Driver
Aramaic Documents of th Fifth Century B.C., rev. ed.

Adolf Neubauer
The Book of Tobit

August Dillman
The Ethiopic Text of 1 Enoch

R. H. Charles
The Apocrypha and Pseudepigrapha of the Old Testament

R. H. Charles
The Book of Enoch

R. H. Charles
The Book of Jubilees

R. H. Charles
The Testaments of the Twelve Patriarchs

R. H. Charles
The Apocalypse of Baruch

H. B. Swete
The Gospel of Peter

Richard Adelbert Lipsius and Max Bonnet
Apocryphal Acts of the Apostles (3 vols.)

Early Babylonian Letters from Larsa

Henry Frederick Lutz

New Bibliography by
K. C. Hanson

Wipf & Stock Publishers
Eugene, Oregon

EARLY BABYLONIAN LETTERS FROM LARSA
Ancient Texts and Translations

ISBN: 1-59752-369-0

The Library of Congress has cataloged an earlier edition of this book:

Lutz, Henry Frederick (1886–)
Early Babylonian letters from Larsa / Henry Frederick Lutz.
Yale Oriental Series. Babylonian Texts, v. 2

New Haven: Yale University Press, 1917.
xiv + 41 p.; LVII pl.; 30 cm.

Plates I-LV, autographed texts; pl. LVI-LVII, half-tone reproductions. "The present volume is the first work published by the Yale university press on the Alexander Kohut Memorial Publication Fund."—Pref. note.
"Names lists": p. 29–37.

1. Assyro-Babylonian Letters. 2. Names, Assyro-Babylonian. I. Title. II. Lutz, Henry Frederick (1886–).

PJ3711.Y3 vol. 2 17025843

Manufactured in the U.S.A.

Series Foreword

The discoveries of documents from the ancient Near Eastern and Mediterranean worlds have altered our modern understanding of those worlds in both breadth and depth. Especially since the mid-nineteenth century, chance discoveries as well as archaeological excavations have brought to light thousands of clay tablets, stone inscriptions and stelae, leather scrolls, codices, papyri, seals, and ostraca.

The genres of these written documents are quite diverse: receipts, tax lists, inventories, letters, prophecies, blessings and curses, dowry documents, deeds, laws, instructions, collections of proverbs, philosophical treatises, state propaganda, myths and legends, hymns and prayers, liturgies and rituals, and many more. Some of them came to light in longfamous cities—such as Ur, Babylon, Nineveh, and Jerusalem—while others came from locations that were previously little-known or unknown—such as Ebla, Ugarit, Elephantine, Qumran, and Nag Hammadi.

But what good are these remnants from the distant past? Why should anyone bother with what are often fragmentary, obscure, or long-forgotten scraps of ancient cultures? Each person will answer those questions for herself or himself, depending upon interests and commitments. But the documents have influenced scholarly research in several areas.

It must first be said that the documents are of interest and importance in their own right, whatever their connections—or lack of them—to modern ethnic, religious, or ideological concerns. Many of them provide windows on how real people lived in the ancient world—what they grew and ate; how they related to their families, business associates, and states; how they were taxed; how and whom they worshiped; how they organized their communities; their hopes and fears; and how they understood and portrayed their own group's story.

They are of intense interest at the linguistic level. They provide us with previously unknown or undeciphered languages and dialects, broaden our range of vocabularies and meanings, assist us in mapping the relationships and developments of languages, and provide examples of loan-words and linguistic influences between languages. A monumental project such as *The Assyrian Dictionary,* produced by the Oriental Institute at the University of Chicago, would have been unthinkable without the broad range of Akkadian resources today.[1] And our study of Coptic and early gospels would be impoverished without the Nag Hammadi codices.[2]

The variety of genres also attracts our interest in terms of the history of literature. Such stories as Athra-hasis, Enumma Elish, and Gilgamesh have become important to the study of world literature. While modern readers may be most intrigued by something with obvious political or religious content, we often learn a great deal from a tax receipt or a dowry document. Hermann Gunkel influenced biblical studies not only because of his keen insights into the biblical books, but because he studied the biblical genres in the light of ancient Near

---

[1] I. J. Gelb et al., editors, *The Assyrian Dictionary of the Oriental Institute of the University of Chicago* (Chicago: Univ. of Chicago Press, 1956–).

[2] James M. Robinson, editor, *The Nag Hammadi Library in English,* 3d ed. (San Francisco: HarperSanFrancisco, 1990).

Eastern texts. As he examined the genres in the Psalms, for example, he compared them to the poetic passages throughout the rest of the Bible, the Apocrypha, the Pseudepigrapha, Akkadian sources, and Egyptian sources.[3] While the Akkadian and Egyptian resources were much more limited in the 1920s and 1930s when he was working on the Psalms, his methodology and insights have had an ongoing significance.

History is also a significant interest. Many of these texts mention kingdoms, ethnic and tribal groups, rulers, diplomats, generals, locations, or events that assist in establishing chronologies, give us different perspectives on previously known events, or fill in gaps in our knowledge. Historians can never have too many sources. The Amarna letters, for example, provide us with the names of local rulers in Canaan during the fourteenth century BCE, their relationship with the pharaoh, as well as the military issues of the period.[4]

Social analysis is another area of fertile research. A deed can reveal economic structures, production, land tenure, kinship relations, scribal conventions, calendars, and social hierarchies. Both the Elephantine papyri from Egypt (fifth century BCE) and the Babatha archive from the Judean desert (second century CE) include personal legal documents and letters relating to dowries, inheritance, and property transfers that provide glimpses of complex kinship relations, networking, and legal witnesses.[5] And the Elephantine documents also include letters to the high priest in Jerusalem from the priests of Elephantine regarding the rebuilding of the Elephantine temple.

Religion in the ancient world was usually embedded in either political or kinship structures. That is, it was normally a function of either the political group or kin-group to which one belonged. We are fortunate to have numerous texts of epic literature, liturgies, and rituals. These include such things as creation stories, purification rituals, and the interpretation of sheep livers for omens. The Dead Sea Scrolls, for example, provide us with biblical books, texts of biblical interpretation, community regulations, and liturgical texts from the second temple period.[6]

Another key element has been the study of law. A variety of legal principles, laws, and collections of regulations provide windows on social structures, economics, governance, property rights, and punishments. The stele of Hammurabi of Babylon (c. 1700 BCE) is certainly the most famous. But we have many more, for example: Ur-Nammu (c. 2100 BCE), Lipit-Ishtar (c. 1850 BCE), and the Middle Assyrian Laws (c. 1150 BCE).

The intention of Ancient Texts and Translations (ATT) is to make available a variety of ancient documents and document collections to a broad range of readers. The series will include reprints of long out-of-print volumes, revisions of earlier editions, and completely

---

[3] Hermann Gunkel, *Einleitung in die Psalmen: Die Gattungen der religiösen Lyrik Israels,* completed by Joachim Begrich, HAT (Göttingen: Vandenhoeck & Ruprecht, 1933). ET = *Introduction to the Psalms: The Genres of the Religious Lyric of Israel,* trans. James D. Nogalski, Mercer Library of Biblical Studies (Macon, Ga.: Mercer Univ. Press, 1998).

[4] William L. Moran, *The Amarna Letters* (Baltimore: Johns Hopkins Univ. Press, 1992).

[5] Bezalel Porten et al., editors, *The Elephantine Papyri in English: Three Millennia of Cross-Cultural Continuity and Change,* Documenta et Monumenta Orientis Antiqui 22 (Leiden: Brill, 1996); Yigael Yadin et al., *The Finds from the Bar Kokhba Period in the Cave of Letters,* 3 vols., Judean Desert Studies (Jerusalem: Israel Exploration Society, 1963–2002) [NB: vols. 2 and 3 are titled *Documents* instead of *Finds*].

[6] Florentino Garcia Martinez, *The Dead Sea Scrolls Translated: The Qumran Texts in English,* 2d ed., trans. Wilfred G. E. Watson (Grand Rapids: Eerdmans, 1996).

new volumes. The understanding of ancient societies depends upon our close reading of the documents, however fragmentary, that have survived.

—K. C. Hanson
Series Editor

Select Bibliography

Alexander, John Bruce. *Early Babylonian Letters and Economic Texts.* Babylonian Inscriptions in the Collection of James B. Nies, Yale University 7. New Haven: Yale Univ. Press, 1943.

Al-Zibari, Akram. *Altbabylonische Briefe des Iraq-Museums.* Köln: Wasmund, 1964.

Cagni, L. *Briefe aus dem Iraq Museum: (TIM II).* Altbabylonische Briefe in Umschrift und Übersetzung 8. Leiden: Brill, 1980.

Clay, Albert T. *Neo-Babylonian Letters from Erech.* Yale Oriental Series, Babylonian Texts 3. New Haven: Yale Univ. Press, 1919.

Cole, Steven W., and Peter Machinist. *Letters from Priests to the Kings Esarhaddon and Assurbanipal.* State Archives of Assyria 13. Helsinki: Helsinki University Press, 1998.

Frankena, R. *Briefe aus dem British Museum (LIH und CT 2–33).* Altbabylonische Briefe in Umschrift und Übersetzung 2. Leiden: Brill, 1966.

———. *Briefe aus der Leidener Sammlung (TLB IV).* Altbabylonische Briefe in Umschrift und Übersetzung 3. Leiden: Brill, 1968.

———. *Briefe aus dem Berliner Museum.* Altbabylonische Briefe in Umschrift und Übersetzung 6. Leiden: Brill, 1974.

Harper, Robert Francis. *Assyrian and Babylonian Letters Belonging to the Kouyunjik Collections of the British Museum.* Chicago: Univ. of Chicago Press, 1892–1914.

Heimpel, Wolfgang. *Letters to the King of Mari: A New Translation, with Historical Introduction, Notes, and Commentary.* Winona Lake, Ind.: Eisenbrauns, 2003.

Kraus, F. R. *Briefe aus dem British Museum: CT 43 und 44.* Altbabylonische Briefe in Umschrift und Übersetzung 1. Leiden: Brill, 1964.

———. *Briefe aus dem Archive des Samas-Hazir: In Paris und Oxford (TCL 7 und OECT 3).* Altbabylonische Briefe in Umschrift und Übersetzung 4. Leiden: Brill, 1968.

———. *Briefe aus dem Istanbuler Museum.* Altbabylonische Briefe in Umschrift und Übersetzung 5. Leiden: Brill, 1972.

———. *Briefe aus dem British Museum (CT 52).* Altbabylonische Briefe in Umschrift und Übersetzung 7. Leiden: Brill, 1977.

———. *Briefe aus kleineren westeuropäischen Sammlungen.* Altbabylonische Briefe in Umschrift und Übersetzung 10. Leiden: Brill, 1985.

Kraus, Paul. *Altbabylonische Briefe aus der vorderasiatischen Abteilung der Preussischen Staatsmuseen zu Berlin.* 2 vols. Mitteilungen der Vorderasiatisch-aegyptischen gesellschaft 35/2, 36/1. Leipzig: Hinrichs, 1931–32.

Kupper, Jean-Robert. *Lettres royales du temps de Zimri-Lim.* Archives royales de Mari 28. Paris: Recherche sur les Civilisations, 1998.

Luukko, Mikko, and Greta van Buylaere. *The Political Correspondence of Esarhaddon.* State Archives of Assyria 18. Helsinki: Helsinki University Press, 2002.

Michalowski, Piotr. *Letters from Early Mesopotamia.* Writings from the Ancient World 3. Atlanta: Scholars, 1993.

Parpola, Simo. *Letters from Assyrian Scholars to the Kings Esarhaddon and Assurbanipal.* 2 vols. Alter Orient und Altes Testament 5/1–2. Kevelaer: Butzon & Bercker, 1970–83.

———. *The Correspondence of Sargon II.* 3 vols. State Archives of Assyria 1, 5, 15. Helsinki: Helsinki University Press, 1987–2001.

Pfeiffer, Robert H. *State Letters of Assyria: A Transliteration and Translation of 355 Official Assyrian Letters Dating from the Sargonid Period (722–625 B.C.).* American Oriental Series 6. New Haven: American Oriental Society, 1935.

Radau, Hugo. *Letters to Cassite Kings from the Temple Archives of Nippur.* Babylonian Expedition of the University of Pennsylvania. Series A: Cuneiform Texts 17/1. Philadelphia: Univ. of Pennsylvania, 1908.

Reynolds, Frances. *The Babylonian Correspondence of Esarhaddon, and Letters to Assurbanipal and Sin-Sarru-Iskun from Northern and Central Babylonia.* State Archives of Assyria 18. Helsinki: Helsinki University Press, 2003.

Soldt, W. H. *Letters in the British Museum.* 2 vols. Altbabylonische Briefe in Umschrift und Übersetzung 12, 13. Leiden: Brill, 1990–94.

Stephens, Ferris J. *Assyrian Letters and Business Documents.* Babylonian Inscriptions in the Collection of James B. Nies, Yale University 6. New Haven: Yale Univ. Press, 1944.

Stol, M. *Letters from Yale.* Altbabylonische Briefe in Umschrift und Übersetzung 9. Leiden: Brill, 1981.

———. *Letters from Collections in Philadelphia, Chicago, and Berkeley.* Altbabylonische Briefe in Umschrift und Übersetzung 11. Leiden: Brill, 1986.

Theis, Johannes. *Altbabylonische Briefe: Teil I.* Leipzig: Pries, 1913.

Ungnad, Arthur. *Babylonian Letters of the Hammurapi Period.* University of Pennsylvania, University Museum, Publications of the Babylonian Section 7. Philadelphia: University Museum, 1915.

Waterman, Leroy. *Royal Correspondence of the Assyrian Empire.* University of Michigan Studies, Humanistic Series 17–20. Ann Arbor: University of Michigan Press, 1930–36.

Whiting, Robert M. Jr. *Old Babylonian Letters from Tell Asmar.* Assyriological Studies 22. Chicago: Oriental Institute of the Univ. of Chicago, 1987.

To My Teacher

PROFESSOR A. T. CLAY, Ph.D., LL.D.

in

Deep Gratitude

This Volume is Dedicated

PREFACE.

In the summer of 1914 the Curator of the Babylonian Collection of Yale University, Professor A. T. Clay, assigned to me the work of publishing letters belonging to the First Dynasty of Babylon. The original plan was that the work should not stop by merely editing the texts, but that with the text-edition there should go hand in hand the transliteration and translation of each autographed letter. My departure from New Haven since then, however, has interfered with the original plan. As the tablets which engage me at present at the Pennsylvania University Museum are of the same general order, i. e., epistolary literature, I hope that time will permit me in a not too distant future to give full transliterations and translations of all the Yale letters here published.

My thanks are due to Professor A. T. Clay for his kind assistance and his valuable suggestions during the preparation of this volume; and it affords me the highest pleasure, as an expression of appreciation and gratitude, to dedicate this volume to him.

Henry Frederick Lutz

TABLE OF CONTENTS.

EARLY BABYLONIAN LETTERS FROM LARSA

INTRODUCTION.

The present volume contains one hundred and fifty-two official and private letters found in the Babylonian Collection of Yale University. These letters, without exception, were written in the classical age of Babylonian history (ca. 2000 B. C.). Most of the tablets, from which the copies were made, are unbaked and a large number are in rather a poor state of preservation. Various reasons may be assigned for this condition, among which is the fact that many of the letters are probably the first drafts, which were preserved as copies for filing purposes. Another reason for their poor preservation will be found in the transient value of letters in general. In most cases after a letter had been read by the recipient, it had accomplished its mission, and little further interest was attached to it; hence was thrown away. Only in those few cases where the sender expressly notified the receiver *tuppi kîl*, i. e. "keep my letter," or as possible evidence, was a letter preserved.

Practically all these letters come from the mounds at Senkereh, which represents the site of the ancient city of Larsa (Ellasar of Gen. 14:1). This is borne out by the fact that most of them were acquired by the Yale Collection together with a large number of business and legal contracts, which bear Larsa dates. A few tablets were added later to the Collection, while the writer was engaged in copying and studying the material. The provenance of them could not be ascertained from the dealers.

In a few cases internal evidence corroborates the above, that the provenance is Senkereh. No. 94:6 betrays its place of origin by the date: ŠÀ MU Ê ^{dingir}IM ŠÀ UD.UNU^{ki} BA-DU, "The year in which the temple of Adad was built in Larsa."[1] The writer of Letter No. 49, as well as of No. 110, is obviously identical with the one of Letter No. 94, as all three letters are addressed *ana bêlia*, "to my lord," for whom Ṣili-Shamash, the writer, discharges in every instance affairs concerning business in grain. The writer's identity in this case would point to Larsa also in regard to Nos. 49 and 110. The evidence in case of Letter No. 143 is plain. The writer, here, informs his addressees, who live in Tubliash, that *Larsa*^{ki} *lu(m) šalim*, "Larsa indeed is well."

[1] Dr. Grice of the Yale Babylonian Seminar, who is studying documents from Larsa, informs me that this date belongs to the reign of Rim-Sin.

These letters are apparently such duplicates of letters, referred to above, which had been preserved in the archives at Larsa for reference. If Prof. Ungnad's conjecture is right that Emutbalum is probably "Gesammtbezeichnung des Besitzstandes von Larsa;" then also Letter No. 134 bears the mark of coming from Larsa. "*Matum*" in line 9 is later on in the letter named "*Iamutbalum.*" The situation pictured in the letter seems to be the following. The writer had made a journey to Iamutbalum and while there, he became involved in a law-suit. This suit was obviously a case of "an individual *versus* the state." This is clear from the verb which is employed: "*matum dububât.*" This condition causes the writer to admonish the addressees not to follow him thither, as had been prearranged, but to remain at home.

Letter No. 6 is an original, which was sent to Larsa. The addressee is Sin-idinnam, who doubtless is to be identified with the "great and loyal feudatory" of Hammurabi. The reason for ascribing this letter to the archives of the well-known governor of Larsa is the fact that Sin-idinnam is asked to render a verdict in a pending law-suit. Sin-idinnam thus is asked in the letter to act as judge, in which capacity he frequently acted.[2]

Letter No. 82 would also bear evidence of coming from Larsa, if the writer, who addresses his letter *ana bêlia*, "to my lord," is, again, the governor Sin-idinnam. In that case "my lord" would be Hammurabi himself. It should be stated, however, that while *ana bêlia* is a form of address of royalty at this period as well as of later periods, most letters with such an address are sent by servants to their masters, subalterns to higher officials, or by women to their husbands.[3] The phrase occurring in lines 22 and 23 of this letter: *ḫi-tu-um a-na pa-ni be-li ú-ul i-pa-ri-ik*, i. e., "crime against my lord has not been committed" (*i-pa-ri-ik*, a defective niphal for *ipparik*), strengthens the supposition that the writer is to be identified with the governor, who again functioned as judge.

The occurrence, also, of the name Balmunamḫe, written also Balmenamḫi, Udbalnamḫe and in the diminutive form, Bala, in Letters No. 7, 13, 77 and 96, is another indication that the material came from Larsa. This name is found very frequently on business documents in the Yale Collection, whose provenance is Larsa.

While the cases are few which corroborate the external evidence of Larsa as the place of discovery, there is, on the other hand, not the least evidence to show that the letters came from any other site.

[2] See King, *Letters and Inscriptions of Hammurabi*, pl. 18, No. 11; pl. 32, No. 19.

[3] See Ungnad, *Babylonian Letters of the Hammurabi Period, UMBS*, Vol. VII, Introduction, p. 10.

In only a few cases can the reign to which these letters belong be determined. This is due to the fact that few names of this period from dated documents, from this section of the country, have been published. Even if we had long lists of names it would still remain a difficult task to ascertain the dates, as family names are very seldom given in letters. In a few cases only can the use of old signs be employed as a criterion to determine the reign, for as Ungnad has correctly observed, "we will find young and old forms of signs even in the same letter, which fact clearly shows, that the old forms are merely artificial ones."[4] As stated above No. 94 is dated in the reign of Rim-Sin. Letters Nos. 6, 19, 32 and 82 can be fixed as belonging to the reign of Hammurabi. Nos. 6 and 82 are letters, the former addressed to, the latter sent by Sin-idinnam, as stated above. Letter No. 19 mentions both Hammurabi and Sin-idinnam, while No. 32 is a letter of the king. Outside of these, no attempt is made to indicate the probable reign of the tablets, as such an endeavor would be too precarious.

Most of the present letters refer to business matters, and seem to have belonged to the archives of the temple. Letters of administrative, judicial, military and purely private or social content, are less frequent among them.

The contents of the letters in only a small number of cases add anything new to the already furnished data of the legal and business contracts. In many cases their contents are even uninteresting. To use Otto Weber's expression[5] in somewhat different meaning, the Babylonian letters are "Kraut- und Ruebenbriefe." But we should expect no more from the antique than from the modern letter. Both are due to the necessity of the moment and their interest generally is but for the moment. They do not belong to the realm of belles-lettres, but nevertheless, for purely linguistic purposes, no one would dispense with this field of "literature."

The following is a list of letters which have come from the same writer, addressed to one and the same addressee.

Nâbi-^{il}Shamash......	^{il}Marduk-nâṣir,	Nos. 11; 14; 125; 127 and 144.
^{il}Anu-mubaliṭ........	Ea-ṣulul-šu,	Nos. 18 and 60.
Idin-Urra............	Sin-mâgir,	Nos. 116; 121 and 128.
Sin-iqîsham..........	Nûr-^{il}Adad,	Nos. 23; 56 and 91(?).
Bêlia................	Ṣili-^{il}Shamash,	Nos. 49; 94 and 110.
Dadâ ù ^{il}Sin-úzili....	Sheib-^{il}Sin,	Nos. 112 and 134.
Bêlshunu............	^{il}Shamash-ḫâṣir,	Nos. 20; 28; 51; 58; 85; 99; 103; 137; 142.

[4] Ungnad, *ibidem*, Introduction, p. 10.

[5] *Literatur der Babylonier und Assyrer*, p. 264.

The addressee of Letter No. 97, who is here named *šabirini,* "our governor," and who receives that letter from Sin-shamuḫ and others, is perhaps the writer of the letter No. 92, namely, Gimillum, who on his part addressed his letter to *Sin-šamuḫ, ilAdad-šarrum, Šunatum, Ṣili-ilDamkina ù madûtim.*[6]

Interesting among the present material is No. 131, as it is the only letter of the lot that has a seal-impression on the tablet itself. In this tablet is also found the only case where the names of witnesses are recorded. No. 130, although no letter, has been added for the sake of convenience. The envelopes of only three letters are preserved, No. 15, 147, and YBC 6826. The envelope of No. 147 has a splendid seal-impression (see Plate LVI). No. 6826 (see Plate LVI) for the present, remains unopened, this being a beautiful example of a sealed letter.

Attention should be called to the writing in Letter No. 1 of the name of the goddess ilIl-Ishtar, perhaps to be read ilIl-Ashirta or ilIl-Ashratu. As the writing occurs twice in line 5, as well as in line 37, there remains no doubt that it is another example of the West-Semitic custom of actually pronouncing אל "god" as a prefix to the names of deities,[7] like El-Shaddai (אל שדי), El-Elyon (אל עליון), ilIlu-we-ir (אלור 'Αλωρος), ilIl-Ḫallabu, ilIl-Kanshan, ilIl-Tammesh and ilIl-Teḫri. The reading of the first *Dingir* sign in this letter for *Anu* or *El* is excluded here, although in the oath-formulas of business and legal documents it is often to be read thus. The position of Shamash in this case as third god in the formula of greeting already excludes the reading: *Anu ilIshtar ilShamash,* etc., since it is the established custom in letters to name Shamash first except, however, when the city god of the writer is introduced in the greeting. This city god takes first place and Shamash follows, but Shamash never takes the third place.

In the forthcoming third part of Vol. XI of *UMBS,* the double determinative for god is also found in a school exercise recording two names. While No. 46 reads: *lù-dingirNisaba,* there occurs in No. 47 the reading: *lù-dingirDingir-Nisaba.* This school tablet clearly differentiates between both divine elements. As the tablet elongs to a series which records Sumerian names it gives the first impression that No. 47 contains the dual form, in consideration of the gloss in *CT* XXV, pl. 6, line 25 and the fact that there were actually two Nisabas, or at least two manifestations of that goddess. But it seems to the writer merely accidental that in this particular case such an explanation might be given by some scholar. It is exceedingly more

[6] That *madûtim* in this connection (79:1; 92:5; 96:4; 97:3) is no personal name, but has the meaning of "and others," is assured by its position, i. e., it always stands at the end of the list of names.

[7] See Clay, *Miscellaneous Inscriptions,* p. 98.

probable that also here the West-Semitic custom has been preserved, and that in spite of the fact that this occurs in a series of school texts of Sumerian personal names. The teacher while writing down as a model the name *Lù-^{dingir}Nisaba*, by some association of thoughts becomes aware of the fact that this name has a West Semitic counterpart and put it down in writing, though not phonetically. No. 47, therefore, is to be read: *Amêl-^{il}Il* plus the name of a West Semitic vegetation god or goddess; if not, what is also probable, the Sumerian name has been directly taken over.

Mention may be made here also of the discovery of the name Abraham in its full form in cuneiform. Professor Ungnad of Jena recently found Babylonian forms of the name Abram, written *A-ba-ra-ma, A-ba-am-ra-ma,* and *A-ba-am-ra-am,*[8] which he regarded as exact reproductions of the patriarch's name. In Letter No. 15, there occurs for the first time the fuller form of the name written *A-ba-ra-ḫa-am.* In discussing the question whether the name was Babylonian or foreign, Ungnad called attention to the second element *rama* as not being found in Babylonian names; and yet he offered two arguments to show that it probably was Babylonian, namely the ending *am* in *abam,* and the fact that the father of his "Abram" bears a good Babylonian name, i. e., Awil-Ishtar. He further gave the probable meaning of the name to be "he loves the father;" the second element being derived from the Babylonian verb *râmu* "to love."[9]

The writer concurs with Ungnad in deriving the form from the Semitic stem *râmu,* but not with the view that the name is Babylonian. In the latter case it could hardly be translated "he loves the father." In form, the second element resembles the permansive, which is not found among the forms from the root *râmu* used in native Babylonian names; e. g., *irâm* (preterite) in *Šarru-napišti-irâm, Ninib-ša-kun-na-i-ra-mu,* or *râ'im* (participle) in *Ra-im-kit-ti, Sin-ra-im-zêr,* etc. The fact is, where the supposed permansive *ram(a)* occurs, the names are generally foreign, e. g., *Ašur-kina-ra-am, Šaḫamil-ra-ma,* etc., which occur in the Cappadocian tablets, *Ra-ma-ilu,* etc., which is West Semitic. The use of the mimmation in connection with the first element ending in the vowel *a,* as in *a-ba-am,* does not imply that it is accusative, but that the scribe heard the pronunciation *aba,* and knew that this was a complete element. As regards the contention that the name is Babylonian because Abram's father's name was Awil-Ishtar, we need only refer to names of father and son in the Murashû Documents.[10] Here we find that *Aq-bi-Ja-a-ma* was the son

[8] *Vorderasiatische Schriftdenkmäler,* Heft VII, 92:6, 13; 198:12, 18.

[9] See *Sunday School Times,* January 22, 1910.

[10] See Clay, *Business Documents of the Murashû Sons, UMBS,* Vol. II.

of *Bau-êṭir* (89:3); *Ba-rik(rak)-ku-Ja-a-ma,* the son of *Bêl-šu-nu* (53:13); *Ma-at-ta-nu-nu-Ja-a-ma,* the son of *Bêl-uballiṭ* (53:12); *Rab-bi-El,* the son of *Nabû-zêr-iddina* (158:21, 22); that is, we find here sons bearing West Semitic names, while the fathers have Babylonian names. This points to mixed marriages, or it shows that the Jews in Babylonia had actually adopted Babylonian names; and later their children were given names from their West Semitic home.

It was possible, as long as the newly found name was not known, to maintain with many scholars that the name Abram (אברם) contains the element רם "high" (compare, e. g., names like אביטוב "my father is good," or *Nabû-nâ'id,* "Nebo is exalted"). Since the appearance, however, of *A-ba-ra-ḫa-am* this explanation must give way to another.

The writer maintains that אברם, *A-ba-ra-ma, A-ba-am-ra-ma, A-ba-am-ra-am,* and the newly found *A-ba-ra-ḫa-am* stand for one and the same name. It is further maintained that they are all foreign renderings of a West Semitic name אברחם, which means "Ab (or the father) has loved."[11] The seemingly Hebrew אברם is really not Hebrew in form, but is rather to be explained as a Babylonian form of אברחם; i. e., the West Semitic רחם has passed into the Babylonian *râmu.* West Semitic, like other foreign names, were written generally as their pronunciation was heard by the Babylonians. The natural Babylonian equivalent of Hebrew אברחם, would be *a-ba-ra-am,* etc., yet the name might have been heard as pronounced with the stronger guttural ח =*ḫ*. Again, this guttural is sometimes found in Babylonian names of West Semitic origin as the reproduction of the much weaker ה; see the examples below. At all events the scribe, who wrote *A-ba-ra-ḫa-am* reproduced more accurately the foreign name, *A-ba-ra-ma,* etc., being Babylonian forms. This leaves the Old Testament name Abraham (written with ה) still to be explained.

It might be argued that *A-ba-ra-ḫa-am* is the Babylonian equivalent of the Hebrew אברהם, as in not a few cases West Semitic ה is represented in the cuneiform writing by *ḫ;* e. g., יהו in *ilJa-a-ḫu-u-la-ki-im, ilJa-ḫu-u-na-ta-nu;* הדד in *Ri-ib-ḫa-ad-da;* יהב in *iaḫabi;* אלוה in *ilaḫi,* etc. But not a single name with רהם as an element in all the tens of thousands known Semitic names has been found. There is also no West Semitic root רהם. The reference to Arabic *rahama* "to sprinkle, to rain steadily, to be numerous," is too precarious to be considered.

It seems to the writer that a reasonable theory of the origin of אברהם is that after the name had been reintroduced in the West in its Babylonian form, the

[11] Compare ירחמאל of the Old Testament written Ιεραμεελ in the LXX.

writing of it was then subject to the usual variation seen in foreign names, and in consequence it was rendered in more than one way, including the orthography with ח (compare the Aramaic רהט for רוץ; and ימה for ימין and רשה for ראשין in the Mesha Inscription). Finally, a narrator or redactor, wishing to find a prophetic significance in the name, introduced the far-fetched play on words (Genesis 17, 5), giving the הם of אברהם a connection with the word המון "multitude."

Translations of Selected Texts.

I. (No. 143)

A letter containing an order for seed and grain.

A-na A-ri-um-wa-qar ù A-bil-^{il}*Šamaš*	To Arium-waqar and Abil-Shamash,
qi- bi- ma	speak:
um-ma Ib-ku-ša-ma	Thus says Ibkusha:—
^{il}*Šamaš ù* ^{il}*Tišpak aš-šu-mi-ia*	May Shamash and Tishpak for my sake
li-ba-al-li-ṭu-ku-nu-ti	preserve your life!
^{il}*Tišpak ù Tupliaš*^{ki} *ša-lim*	Tishpak and Tupliash are well.
Larsa^{ki}*·lu(m) ša-lim*	(May) Larsa indeed be well.
ki-ma ti-di-a-a	There is seed and grain,
i-na Tupliaš^{ki} *âli*^{ki}	as you know,
zi-ru-um ù še-um i-ba-aš-ši	in Tupliash, the city.
ša $1\frac{1}{3}$ *šiqlu kaspim*	Take out from
bi-ti ka-ri	the granary
šu-ta-ṣi-a-am-ma	a $1\frac{1}{3}$ shekels of silver worth,
šu-bi-la-nim	and send it.

II. (No. 7)

A request to abstain from giving occasion for legal proceedings until the arrival of the writer.

A-na Bal-a	To Bala,
qi- bi- ma	say as follows:—
um-ma Ku-ub-bu-ti-ia-ma	Thus says Kubbutia:
^{il}*Šamaš li-ba-al-li-ṭu-ka*	May Shamash keep thee healthy!
a-di a-al-la-ka-ak-kum	Until I come to thee,

^{m}*Ta-ri-ba-tum*	do not give Taribatum an occasion
*la tu-da-ab-ba-a[b]**	for legal proceedings.

III. (No. 106)

The writer announces that he has taken notice of the content of a letter written to him, and asks that flour, garments and oil be sent to him.

A-na Si-zi-i ù At-ti-ia	To Sizî and Attia,
qi- bi- ma	speak:—
um-ma Ibiq-nâr-kim-ḫi-ma	Thus says Ibiq-nâr-kimḫi:
^{il}*Šamaš ù* ^{il}*Marduk li-ba-al-li-ṭu-ku-nu-ti*	May Shamash and Marduk preserve your life!
aš-šum um-ma at-tu-nu-ma	Concerning that which you wrote:
a-ḫa-ka tu-ur-da-am-ma	"Send for thy brother so that
lu-ut-ta-ši-ka	he may assist thee," (and) "a man
a-wi-lum ú-nu-ut ekallim	has destroyed the vessels of
ú-ḫa-li-iq-ma	the temple and
1 šiqlam kaspim it-ti ša-su-ú[1]	took 1 shekel of silver
il-qi-ma	by robbery."
um-ma a-na-ku-ma a-pu-ul	I reply as follows: I have taken notice.
i-na eqli(-li)-ia še-um	That grain is not in my
ša-tu ú-ul i-ba-ši	field.
60 qa qêmam šu-bi-lam[2]	Send me 60 *qa* of flour.
ṣu-ba-ti ša ma-aḫ-ri-ku-nu-ma	(Regarding) my garments, which are with you,
e-ri-ši-ia a-ta-na-la-ak	I come continually with my request:

* *tudabbab* could also be translated "Do not sue." The translation above, however, is to be preferred, cf. German Zur Klage veranlassen.

[1] *liqu,* in the language of the Code of Hammurabi, is construed with *itti* of the person of whom something is taken, e. g., *kaspam itti tamqarim ilqi,* i. e., "he has taken money from the merchant." In consideration of this fact one is tempted to translate *šasû* in analogy to the meaning which the Semitic שָׂסָה, pl. שֹׂסִים has received in Egyptian. Here we meet with the interesting fact, that the Egyptian (due undoubtably to the low esteem in which the Asiatics were held by them, and who rendered the Semitic loanword by *šꜣśw,*) gave to the word the meaning of "nomads, beduins" (see, Mueller, *Asien und Europa,* p. 131). While the Babylonian syntax of the period of the First Dynasty would favor a similar translation, it is inconceivable, but not entirely improbable, that the Babylonians would employ the word "plunderer, robber" as a designation of the desert-dwellers.

[2] *Šu-bi-la-nim* should here be expected.

lu-ba-ar-tam iš-ṫa-a-at	Send me
šu-bi-la-nim	one robe!
a-aḫ-ku-nu e-[li]-ia la ta-na-di	Do not be negligent toward me!
ú-la-nu ba-a-ba a-ḫa-am	You have always
i-šu-ú	another excuse.
$\frac{1}{2}$ *qa šamnam šu-bi-[la]-nim*	Send me a half of a *qa* of oil.

IV. (No. 134)

The letter communicates that the writer has become implicated in a court proceeding. He requests the addressees not to start on a journey that year.

A-na Da-da-a	To Dadâ,
ù ^{il}Sin-ú-zi-li	and Sin-uzili,
qi- bi- ma	speak as follows:—
um-ma Še-ib-^{il}Sin-ma	Thus says Šeib-Sin:
^{il}Šamaš ù ^{il}Ezinu	May Shamash and Ezinu for my sake
aš-šum-ia li-ba-al-li-ṭu-ku-nu-ti	keep you well!
iš-tu al-li-ka-am	Since I have gone,
du-bu-ba-ku	I am engaged in a law-suit and the
ù ma-tu-um du-bu-ba-at	country is (likewise) implicated in a legal proceeding.
ša-at-ta-am la ta-la-ka-ni	You shall not go this year,
ù a-na Ja-mu-ut-ba-li	nor shall you journey
la tu-ra-da-ni	to Jamutbalum.
a-di a-ša-pa-ra-ku-nu-ti	Until I write to you,
la ta-la-ka-ni	you shall not come.
ù a-na ali^{ki} šu-lim̊	So return safely(?)
ta-a-ar-ta-am ri-ša-a	to the city.
a-na ki-zi-ku-nu la te-gi-a	Do not be neglectful to your companion.
i-na ga-ti-ku-nu	Do not leave the one-sixth of a
kaspam $\frac{1}{6}$ šiqlu la te-zi-ba-ni	shekel of silver in your hands.

V. (No. 121)

An order for reed-baskets.

[A-n]a I-din-Ur-ra	To Idin-Urra
qi- bi- ma	speak as follows:—
um-ma Sin-ma-gir-ma	Thus says Sin-mâgir:

2 pisannu^{ṣun}	Give
a-na ^{il}*Šamaš-li-wi-ir*	to Shamash-liwir
i-di-in	2 reed-baskets.

VI. (No. 92)

A letter concerning the distribution of profit-shares.

A-na Sin-ša-mu-uḫ	To Sin-shamuḫ,
^{il}*Adad-šar-rum*	Adad-šarrum,
^{m}*Šu-na-tum*	Shunatum,
^{m}*Ṣili-*^{il}*Dam-ki-na*	Ṣili-Damkina,
ù ma-du-tim	and others,
qi- bi- ma	speak:—
um-ma Gi-mil-lum	Thus says Gimillum:
^{il}*Šamaš li-ba-al-li-iṭ-ku-nu-ti*	May Shamash preserve your life!
ki-ma ta-aš-ta-na-am-[mi-e]	As you have heard,
iš-tu û-mi arḫim 2^{kam}	since the second month
ṣabê^{meš} *a-ḫi-a-tim*	my master has told me to distribute
ša i-ba-aš-šu-ú	to the men the equal shares of the
be-li za-za-am iq-bi-i-ma	profits which are on hand.
ṣabê^{meš} *a-ḫi-a-tim ša i-ba-aš-šu-ú*	So I put the equal shares of the
i-na ga-bi be-li-ia	profits which are on hand, before the
aṣ-ṣu-uk-zu-nu-ši-im	men, on account of the order of my lord.
aš-šu-mi-ku-nu	On account of you
be-li za-za-am iq-bi-a-am-ma	my lord has told me to divide up.
a-na be-li-ia ki-a-am aq-bi	And to my lord I spoke in this fashion:
um-ma a-na-ku-ma ṣabê^{meš} *a-ḫi-a-tim*	"Let the men take the equal
ša i-ba-aš-šu-ú li-il-qu-ú-ma	shares of the profits which are on hand.
LÙ LIBIT^{ki} *ú-ul a-na-di-iš-šu-nu-ti*	But the men of the brickyard, I do
ù LÙ LIBIT^{ki} *iš-tu ar-ḫim* 2^{kam}	not give them." So I hold the brick-
ú-ṣa-ab-ba-at-šu-nu-ti	layers since two months.
a-li-a-nim-ma	Come up and
a-wa-ti-ku-nu ša na-ši-a-tu-nu	your case, which you have,
ma-ḫar ardê^{meš} *šarrim šu-uk-na*	establish before the servants of the king.

VII. (No. 124)

A request to buy three slaves for the writer.

A-na A-ḫu-wa-qar	To Aḫu-waqar,
qi- bi- ma	speak:—
um-ma A-ḫu-ni-ma	Thus says Aḫuni:
tup-pi an-ni-a-am	When thou seest
i-na a-ma-ri-im	this letter,
a-nu-um-ma	then I despatch
^{il}*Šamaš-ilu*	Shamash-ilu
a-na ṣi-ri-ka	unto
at-tar-dam	thy presence.
1 ma-na kaspim	Take the
[ub-ba-la]-kum	one mine of silver
li-qi-e-ma	he is bringing thee,
ša 1 ma-na kaspim	and for the one mine of silver
1 ŠAG.WARAD	buy
2 ŠAG.GEM	one male slave and
ša-ma-am-ma	two female slaves,
a-na DUG.GAR^{ki}	and to the town DUG.GAR,
a-na ṣi-ri-ia	unto me,
šu-ri-a-am	cause (them) to be brought,
ab-bu-tum	please.

VIII. (No. 22)

Concerning a cargo of sand.

A-na Ṣi-li-........	To Ṣili-........,
qi- bi- [ma]	speak:—
um-ma Gi-m[il-lu]m-ma	Thus says Gimillum:
ku-nu-uk-ki-ia an-ni-a-am	When thou seest
i-na a-ma-ri-ka	my sealed letter
1 ^{is}*elippi-ka i-di-im-ma*	give one of thy ships
e-pi-ri it-ti-šu	and let sand be brought
li-ši-a-am	in it unto me.

IX. (No. 25)

A letter transmitting the decision of the court at Babylon in matters referring to a dowry.

A-na Mu-ḫa-ad-du-um	To the Muḫaddu,
qi- bi- ma	speak:—
um-ma daianê^{meš} *Bâbili*^{ki}*-ma*	Thus say the judges of Babylon:
^{il}*Šamaš ù* ^{il}*Marduk li-ba-al-li-ṭu-ku-nu-ti*	May Shamash and Marduk preserve your life!
aš-šum di-nim ša Ilu-šu-i-bi-[šu]	As to matters pertaining to the law-
ù Ma-at-ta-tum	suit of Ilušu-ibišu and Mattatum:
a-wa-ti-šu-nu ni-mu-ur	We have examined their case.
di-nam ki-ma ṣi-im-da-at be-li-ni	Judgment according to the law of
nu-ša-ḫi-iṣ-ṣu-nu-ti-ma	our lord we have rendered them.
mi-im-ma nu-du-un-na-a-am	The entire dowry,
ša Ma-at-ta-tum	which Mattatum
a-na ma-ar-ti-ša id-di-nu-ma	gave to her daughter,
[a-n]a bit Ilu-šu-i-bi-šu	when she brought her to the
[ú]-se-ri-b[u-ši]	house of Ilushu-ibishu,
a-na Ma-at-ta-tum	we have said must revert
tu-ur-ram ni-iq-bi	to Mattatum.
redam it-ti-ša ni-it-tar-dam	We despatch a sheriff to her.
mi-im-ma ba-al-ṭa-am ša i-na-an-na	Let them give
in-na-aṭ-ṭa-lu	unto Mattatum
a-na Ma-at-ta-tum	everything in such good condition
li-id-di-nu	as it is now beheld.

X. (No. 139)

A reply in which the writer expresses his willingness to redeem a ship.

A-na Da-an-ilu ù In-bi-Sin	To Dân-ilu and Inbi-Sin,
qi- bi- ma	speak as follows:—
um-ma Sa-ni-i-ma	Thus says Sanî:
^{il}*Šamaš ù* ^{il}*Marduk li-ba-al-li-ṭu-ku-nu-ti*	May Shamash and Marduk keep you well!
aš-šum elippim ša ta-aq-bi-a-am	In regard to the ship about which

elippam a-na be-li ta-pa-ṭa-ar	thou hast spoken to me: "Redeem the ship for the possessor,"
tup-pi uš-ta-bi-la-ak-kum	I have sent unto thee my letter.
me-ḫi-ir tup-pi-ia šu-bi-lam-ma	Send me an answer to my letter.
a-na tu-ku-ul-ti-ka	In your trust
elippam a-na be-li-ša	I may return the ship
lu- te- ir	to its possessor.

XI. (No. 36)

A letter containing a demand for ships and sailors.

A-na a-bi-ia	To my father,
qi- bi- ma	speak:—
um-ma A-ba-a-ma	Thus says Abâ:
[il]Šamaš li-ba-al-li-iṭ-ka	May Shamash keep thee healthy!
a-nu-um-ma [m]I-din-EN.MUN	I, now, despatch
aṭ-ṭar-da-ak-kum	Idin-ENMUN unto thee.
[is]elippê[meš] 20 gur	Cause to bring unto me ships
ga-du ra-ka-bi-	of 20 kors tonnage
ši-na	with
na-ṭu-ti	their
a-na ṣi-ri-ia	able
šu-ra-am	crews.

XII. (No. 50)

Concerning the adoption of a youth, who had been disinherited, and who had deserted his parental home.

A-na Mu-na-wi-rum	To Munawirum,
qi- bi- ma	speak:—
um-ma Ti-ša-na-tum-ma	Thus says Tishanatum:
aš-šum ša ta-aš-pur-am um-ma at-ta-ma	In regard to that which thou hast written:
Um-mi-na-di-tum ṣu-ḫa-ra-am	"Ummi-naditum took the boy
a-na li-qu-tim il-qi-e-ma	for adoption.
ṣu-ḫa-rum šu-ú zi-k[i-i]r-ši-ma	That boy calls her (mother)!
20 ši-bu-ut a-lim ú-pa-aḫ-ḫi-ir-šum-ma	20 city-elders I assembled for him;

a-wa-a-ti-šu ma-aḫ-ri-šu-nu aš-ku-un-ma	then I established his case in their presence."
aš-šum ṣu-ḫa-[ri-im] šu-ú zi-ki-ir šu-ú	As to this youth's proclamation,
iš-tu šattim 3^{kam} i-na aḫ-ḫu-sum	(I reply): I had disinherited him
at-ta-si-iḫ-šu	three years ago in favor of his
i-na-an-na il-li-ik	brother. Now he has gone.
ú-qa-al-li-il-ma	He has made light of (it).
um-ma ša-pi-ir nârim-ma	The governor of the canal-zone
a-li-ik-ma narkabtam a-pu-ul	(wrote): "Come and return the wagon.
ša ta-aš-pur-am	That which thou hast written to me
a-na a-wi-lim aq-bi-ma	I have told the man,
tup-pu-um ša a-wi-lim	and the letter of the man
a-na I-din-Sin it-[ta-a]l-kam	has gone to Idin-Sin.
ú-ul i-ta-ar-ma	He shall not return."
aš-šum ṣu-ḫa-ri-im šu-a-ti	I shall not bring legal proceedings
ú-ul ú-da-ab-ba-ab-ka	against thee in matters referring to that youth.

XIII. (No. 110)

A statement in reference to different sales of grain.

A-na be-li-ia	To my lord,
qi- bi- ma	speak:—
um-ma Ṣi-li-^{il}Šamaš-ma	Thus says Ṣili-Shamash:
aš-šum še-e-im ša alu Qi-iš-ra-^{il}E-a	In reference to the grain of the city of Qishra-Ea,
ša Sin-ma-gir ù Ilu-šu-ib-ni-[šu]	which Sin-magir and Ilushu-ibnishu
il-qu-ú ša ta-aš-pu-ra-am	bought, about which thou hast written to
i-nu-ú-ma ^{m}Ġi-mi-lum	me at the time when Gimilum made a
ni-ik-ka-az-zi-šu-nu i-pu-šu	settlement of their account:
30 še gur at-ti-iš-šu-nu-ši-i-im	I brought them 30 kors of grain,
ù i-na bit ^{m}Nu-ur-^{il}Adad	and from the house of Nûr-Adad,
ta-aq-bi-a-am-ma 20 gur a-na e-ṣi-di-im	thou hast told me, went out
10 gur a-na ši-pi-ir kirim	for them 20 kors during the harvest
ú-ṣi-e-šu-nu-ši-i-im	(and) 10 kors for garden-work,
60 še gur li-qu-ú	(thus) receiving 60 kors of grain.

XIV. (No. 8)

A grain order for troops.

A-na Šu-nu-um-ilu	To Šunum-ilu,
qi- bi- ma	speak:—
um-ma Šu-mu-um-li-ib-ši-ma	Thus says Shumum-libshi:
^{il}*Šamaš li-ba-al-li-ṭu-ka*	May Shamash keep thee well!
120 qa še-a-am	Give
a-na I-li-i-din-nam	unto Ili-idinnam
i-di-in	120 *qa* of grain.
še-um a-na ṣa-bu-tim	The grain (is) for the troops.
la ta-ka-la-šu	Do not withhold it.

XV. (No. 102)

An order for wool.

A-na Mu-na-wi-rum	To Munawirum,
qi- bi- ma	speak:—
um-ma Sin-šar-ru-um	Thus say Sin-sharrum,
A-bil-ja-tum	Abil-jatum
ù I-din-nam-ma	and Idinnam:
^{il}*Šamaš li-ba-al-li-iṭ-ka*	May Shamash grant thee life!
a-nu-um-ma a-na Sin-ma-gir	We, now, send for Sin-mâgir
ù Be-li-ja-šu	and
ni-iš-tap-ra-am	Bêlijashu.
it-ti-šu-nu	Join
i-zi-iz-ma	them and
šipatu^{sun} *ša 2 šiqlu kaspim*	purchase wool for
li-qi-e-ma	two shekels of silver.
kaspam a-na Sin-e-ri-ba-am	Give the money
i-di-in	to Sin-êribam.
la tu-ur-ra-ak-šu	Do not put him off.

XVI. (No. 3)

Containing a request to take care of a cargo of grain, which will soon arrive.

A-na .... *ù*	To X and Y,
qi- bi- ma	speak:—
um-ma Lu-mur-ša-^{il}*Marduk-ma*	Thus says Lûmur-sha-Marduk:—

^{il}Šamaš li-ba-al-li-ṭu-ku-nu-ti	May Shamash keep you healthy!
aš-šum še-e-im ša ŠA-Malaḫu^{ki}	Concerning the grain of ŠA-Malaḫu,
a-di iš-tu i-na-an-na ûmu 2^{kam}	as soon as the ship arrives
elippum i-sa-an-ni-ga-am	in two days from now,
a-na še-e-im šu-a-ti	do not be negligent
la te-e-gi	in regard to that grain.
pi-ḫa-at še-e-im šu-a-ti e-li-ku-nu-ma	The responsibility of that grain rests upon you, and
la ki-ma aq-bu-ku-nu-ši-im	(it is) not as I had told you.
a-wi-li-e e-is-ḫa-a-nim[1]	The men have ordered (it).

XVII. (No. 12)

Concerning the payment of money.

A-na Sin-li-wi?-ir?	To Sin-liwir,
qi- bi- ma	speak:—
um-ma I-li-ra-bi-ma	Thus says Ili-rabi:
aš-šum ta-aš-pu-ra-am	Concerning that which
um-ma at-ta-a-ma	thou hast written:
i-nu-u-ma a-na Ra-bi-kum^{ki}	"At the time when thou
ta-al-la-ku-ma	goest to Rabikum
šu-up-ra-am-ma 10 šiqlu kaspim	write to me and I shall send unto
[uš]-ta-bi-la-kum	thee the 10 shekels of silver."
iš-tu i-na-an-na a-na ûmi 5^{kam}	Five days hence
a-na Ra-bi-kum^{ki}	my face is turned
pa-nu-ia ša-ak-nu	to Rabikum.
a-nu-um-ma ^{il}Šamaš-ra-bi	I, now, despatch
a-na ṣi-ri-ka	Shamash-rabi
at-ṭar-dam	unto thee.
10 šiqlu kaspim šu-bi-lam-ma	Send me the 10 shekels of silver.

XVIII. (No. 149)

Concerning the purchase of a female slave.

A-na A-bu-wa-qar	To Abu-waqar,
qi- bi- ma	speak:—
um-ma A-ḫu-wa-qar-ma	Thus says Aḫu-waqar:

[1] Mistake for *isḫûnim* (*?*).

aš-šum am-tim	In regard to a female slave
ša ta-aš pu-ra-am	about whom thou hast written to me
ša um-ma at-ta-a-ma	as follows:
a-na ṣi-ir Ṣi-li-^{il}*Adad*	"Go
a-li-ik-ma	to Ṣili-Adad and
am-tam li-di-kum	let him give thee a female slave."
al-li-ik-šum-ma	I went to him and
ụm-ma a-na-ku-ú-ma	(reply) in the following manner:
. . .-ik?-ta?-. . .-šu-. . .	. . . .
ša A-bu-wa-qar	that Abu-waqar
iš-pu-ur-ra-an-ni	wrote to me:
am-tam id-nam	"Purchase a slave-maid."
um-ma šu-ú-ma	He (answered):
i-pa-la-an-ni-ma	"He shall pay me.
a-na be-el am-tim	I did not (yet) go
la al-li-kam	to the slave-owner.
am-tam a-na ma-am-ma-an	And the slave-maid I shall give
ú-ul a-na-ad-di-in	to no one (else)."
ma-ar ši-ib-ri-ka	Send over
šu-bi-ra-am-ma	thy messenger,
am-tam li-di-nam	and let him purchase the slave-maid.
ab-bu-tum	Please.

XIX. (No. 94)

A report of the weight of certain grain.

A-na be-li-ia	To my lord
qi- bi- ma	speak:—
um-ma Ṣi-li-^{il}*Šamaš-ma*	Thus says Ṣili-Shamash:
še-um ša dimti ka-at-tim	The grain at Dimti Kattim
5 gur ib-ba-a-ši	is 5 kors.
ŠÀ MU Ê ^{dingir}*IM ŠÀ UD.UNU*^{ki} *BA-DU*	In the year in which the temple of Adad in Larsa was built.

XX. (No. 13)

An order for the sale of grain.

A-na Na-bi-^{il}*Gu-la*	To Nâbi-Gula,
ù Bal-mu-nam-ḫe	and Balmunamhe,
qi- bi- ma	speak:—
um-ma Sin-a-ia-ba-aš-ma	Thus says Sin-aiabash:
^{il}*Šamaš li-ba-al-li-iṭ-ku-nu-ti*	May Shamash keep you well!
^{m}*Ig-mil-Sin*	Igmil-Sin
ù Ba-ak-kum rê'um	and Bakkum, the shepherd, have
ka-ni-ki it-ba-lu-ni-ku-nu-ši-im	brought you my sealed document.
a-na bi-i ka-ni-ki	According to the wording of the document
še-am i-na še-am niši I-din-ja-tum	take out the grain of the supply
šu-ṣi-a	of the people of Idinjatum.
šum-ma še-um i-na še-am niši I-din-ja-[tum]	If the supply of grain of the
la i-ba-aš-ši	people of Idinjatum is not on hand,
i-na še-am niši ^{il}*Marduk-la-ma-za-šu sukallu*	(then) give out some of the
šu-ṣi-a	grain of the people of Marduk-lamazashu the supervisor.

XXI. (No. 10)

A request to act as a caravan leader.

A-na Wa-tar-^{il}*Šamaš*	To Watar-Shamash,
qi- bi- ma	speak:—
um-ma Ilu-šu-ib-ni-šu-ma	Thus says Ilushu-ibnishu:
^{il}*Šamaš li-ba-al-li-iṭ-ka*	May Shamash keep thee healthy!
a-nu-um-ma a-na Sin-mu-uš-ta-al	I, now, send through Sin-mushtal
tup-pi uš-ta-bi-lam	my letter.
tamqarê^{meš} *ša il-li-ku-nim*	The merchants who have come,
pa-ni-šu-nu	lead,
ṣa-ab-ta-am-ma	and let them set out
a-la-kam li-pu-šu-nim	on the journey.

XXII. (No. 83)

A request for immediate removal of oxen and sheep, which is probably to be brought into close connection with the result of an oracle mentioned, which may have predicted an hostile incursion, a flood or an outbreak of a plague among cattle in a certain district.

A-na Û-bar-ru-um	To Ubarrum,
qi- bi- ma	speak:—
um-ma Awêl-^{il}*Nannar*	Thus says Awêl-Nannar
ma-ru-ka-a-ma	thy son:
a-na Ilu-šu-i-bi-šu ba-ri-im	I wrote to
aš-tu-ur-ma	Ilushu-ibishu, the diviner,
um-ma šu-ú-ma	and he (replied):
a-na ^{il}*Nin-giš-zi-da a-tu*	"They sent to Ningishzida,
iš-pu-ur-ma um-ma šu-ma	the seer. He (said):
i-na ši-ri-im a-mu-ur-ma	"I beheld the oracle.
ši-ru-um za-ḫi-il	The oracle is dreadful."
alpê^{šun} *ù ṣenu*^{šun}	They shall remove
a-na kišad nâr mê Enlil-la	the oxen and the sheep to the
i-na-za-ḫu	canal Me-Ellil (water of Ellil)
alpê^{šun} *uš-ḫa-zu*	The oxen ....
a-šar wa-aš-ba-a-ta	may remain
li-zi-zu	where thou art.
ù mi-di an-ni-ki-a-am	Knowledge shall be to
i-ba-aš-ka-a-ma	thee at once.
al-pi a-na a-li-im	The oxen I .... to the city
a-aš-im-ma i-na-za-ḫu-ma	they shall (also) remove.
pu-ur-tum i-ḫa-li-ik	"A young cow has strayed away."
al-kam-ma pu-ur-ta-am	Well then, restrain the young cow
pu-ru-us-ma ta-ru	repeating (it).
ab-bu-tum	Please!
a-wa-tum da-an-na	The matter is urgent.

XXIII. (No. 114)

An inquiry concerning sheep which had been ordered away from a certain field the governor of the canal-zone.

A-na Warad-^{il}*Šamaš*	To Warad-Shamash,
qi- bi- ma	speak:—

um-ma Wa-tar-^{il}*Šamaš-ma*	Thus says Watar-Shamash:
^{il}*Šamaš ù* ^{il}*Nergal*	May Shamash and Nergal
li-ba-al-li-ṭu-ka	preserve thy life!
aš-šum eqlim$^{(lim)}$ *ša Li-bi-it-*. . . .	Concerning the field of Libit-. . . .
ki-a-am iq-bi-a-am	He spoke like this:
um-ma šu-ú-ma	"From
iš-tu ša-pi-ir na-ri-im	the governor of the canal-zone
ú-lam-mi-id	he learned:
a-na li-ib-bi	Let the neglected sheep
eqlim li-zu	be taken from the midst
ṣenu^{šu}[^{n} *la in-na-da-a*]	of the field."
ṣu-ḫa-[*ru*] *i-pu-ul-šu-*[*ma*]	The boy
um-ma šu-ú-ma	answered him:
mi-im-ma ú-ul li-zu-[*šu-nu-ti*]	"Nothing may take them away."
tup-pi uš-ta-bi-[*la-ak-kum*]	I send thee my letter.
šum-ma i-na ki-i[*t-tim*]	If, in truth,
a-ḫi at-[*ta*]	thou art my brother,
me-ḫi-ir tup-pi-[*ia*]	then send me
ša iš-tu ša-pi-ir na-ri-[*im*]	an answer to my letter,
iq-bu-ma	what was said by the governor of the canal-zone
ṣenu^{šun} *la in-na-da-a*	of the
šu-bi-lam	neglected sheep.

XXIV. (No. 6)

A plaintiff's statement to the judge that the defendant had entirely complied to his demands.

A-na Sin-i-din-nam	To Sin-idinnam,
qi- bi- ma	speak:—
um-ma ^{il}*Marduk-mu-ša-lim-ma*	Thus says Marduk-mushalim:
^{il}*Šamaš ù* ^{il}*Marduk li-ba-al-li-ṭu-ka*	May Shamash and Marduk preserve thy life!
ki-ma ti-du ú-ul ^{il}*Šamaš-rê'u-ti-i-im*(?)	As thou knowest Shamash-rê'utim not
e-bi-iš ṣi-bu-ti-ia	fulfilling my demand,
i-nu-ma a-ša-pa-ru-šum[1]	when I wrote to him

[1] Mistake for: *aš-pu-ra-šum*.

ṣi-bu-ti ma-di-iš i-pu-us	he fully complied with my claim.
a-wa-ti-šu ina maḫ-ri-ka	Let his case be established
li-iš-ku-un-ma	in thy presence, and render judg-
di-nam ki-ma ṣi-im-da-at be-li-ia	ment unto him in just manner accord-
i-ša-ri-iš šu-ḫi-iz-zu	ing to the law of my lord.

XXV. (No. 87)

A request to send a young man.

A-na Na-bi-^{il}Šamaš	To Nabi-Shamash,
qi- bi- ma	speak:—
um-ma ^{il}Adad-ri-im-i-li-ma	Thus says Adad-rîm-ili:
^{il}Šamaš li-ba-al-li-iṭ-ka	May Shamash keep thee well!
[an]-nu-um I-li-gim-la-an-ni	This Ili-gimlanni
[at]-ṭar-da-ak-kum	I despatch unto thee.
ṣu-ḫa-ra-[am]	Send me
it-ti I-li-gim-la-an-ni	a young man
ṭu-ur-da-am	with Ili-gimlanni.

XXVI. (No. 70)

An assurance that the addressee shall not suffer loss for disputed grain.

[A-n]a ^{il}Šamaš-li-wi-ir	To Shamash-liwir,
qi- bi- ma	speak:—
[um-ma] I-li-i-qi-ša-am-ma	Thus says Ili-iqisham:
^{il}[Šamaš] ù [^{il}Marduk] li-ba-al-li-ṭu-ka	May Shamash and Marduk keep thee well!
aš-šum [še] ša I-bi-^{il}Šamaš aḫu-ni	Concerning the grain of Ibi-Shamash, our brother,
ta-aš-pur-am	thou hast written to me.
ki-ma ti-du-ú a-na še-im an-ni-im	As thou knowest for that grain
du-ub-bu-ba-a-ku-ma	I have gone to law, but
ú-ul i-pu-uš-šu	he has not complied to it.
iš-tu i-na-an-na ûmi 2	Two days hence,
[la]-ma aṭ-ṭar-da-am	before I shall send,
[še]-am a-ap-pa-aš-šu[1]	I shall pay him the grain.
mi-im-ma la ta-na-zi-iq	In no manner shalt thou suffer loss.

[1] Assimilation of *l* to following *s*; *a-ap-pa-al-šu*.

XXVII. (No. 81)

A request to send a bronze pot.

A-na Ba-ba-a	To Babâ,
qi- bi- ma	speak:—
um-ma Mu-na-wi-rum-ma	Thus says Munawirum:
^{il}*Šamaš ù* ^{il}*Marduk da-ri-iš û-mi*	May Shamash and Marduk for eternal
li-ba-al-li-ṭu-ki	days keep thee well!
a-nu-um-ma Lu-mur-ša-^{il}*Marduk*	I, now, despatch
aṭ-ṭar-dam	Lûmur-sha-Marduk.
1 URUDU ŠUN šu-bi-li-im	Send me one bronze pot.
a-na-ku kaspam URUDU ŠUN	I shall restore unto thee the
ú-ta-ra-ak-ki	money for the bronze pot.
a-na-ku i-na šu-li-mi	I (for the present) am straitened
ka-la-a-ku	in my circumstances.
aš-šum i-na ki-it-ti-im*	If thou truly
ta-ra-am-mi-in	dost love me,
1 URUDU ŠUN šu-bi-li-im	(then) send me one bronze pot.

XXVIII. (No. 15)

Contains an appeal to good sisterly relation, a complaint for not having granted a reduction in price, a reminder of unfulfilled promises, a willingness on the part of the writer to furnish a certain thing, and an announcement that he despatches someone to get drink and food.

A-na El-me-šum	To Elmeshum,
qi- bi- ma	speak:—
um-ma Si-ru-um-ma	Thus says Sirum:
^{il}*Šamaš ù* ^{il}*TAK Ê-ša-ra*[1] *aš-šum-ia*	May Shamash and TAK of Êshara for my sake
da-ri-iš û-mi li-ba-al-li-ṭu-ki	preserve thy life for eternal days!
at-ḫu-ta-am ki-a-am šu-uk-ni-ma	Establish in this fashion the sisterly relation,
lu ša iš-tu ṣi-iḫ-ḫi-ri-nu-ma	for we have grown up together

* Probably mistake for *šumma*.

[1] *Ê-ša-ra* = *Ê-šar-ra* (Br. 6265) compare: *Ninib pir êšara;* KB III: 162; VI: II; = BA II 203; also comp. KB IV p. 80 Col. IV l. 1. *Êšar(r)a* is an epithet which the Sumerians applied to "*irṣitu*", earth; i. e. "Das Welthaus; the house of totality.

iš-te-ni-eš ni-ir-bu-ú	since we were small.
iš-tu i-lam ta-ar-ši-i[2]	Thou hast acquired since a protective genius[2]
ma-ti-ma i-na šimim 15 še kaspim	Not at all didst thou reduce the
šu-mi ú-ul ta-aḫ-ṣu-ṣi	price of 15 she of silver,
ù ti-ma-li i-nu-ma ta-li-ki-im	but, yesterday, I took Aba-raḫam,
A-ba-ra-ḫa-am el-qi-e-ma	when thou hadst come.
a-di te-ki-mi-in-ni	Not until thou hadst overcharged me
ú-ul ta-am-gu-ri	didst thou comply.
um-ma at-ti-ma ul-la-nu-um	Thou (hast said): "In the future
ḫa-at-ta-am dam-qa-am	I shall send unto thee good ....
ù ka-ta-am ú-ša-ba-la-kum	and ....
ú-ul šu-ta-bi-li-im[3]	Thou didst not cause (it) to be sent.
ù ki-a-am aq-bi-ki um-ma a-na-ku-ma	But as I have told thee I (say again)
a-wi-lum A-bi-^{il}Amurrum ša iḫ-zu-ki[4]	"If the patrician Abi-Amurrum, who
šum-ma ^{iṣ}a-am-ri-e[5] *ḫa-še-iḫ*	took thee, needs beds,
li-iš-[pu]-ra-am-ma 5 ^{iṣ}a-am-ri-e[5]	then let him write to me, and I may
lu-ša-bi-la-aš-šu	send him 5 beds.
a-nu-um-ma it-ti elippim ša-an-nim	I, now, despatch with another ship
a-wi-lam aṭ-ṭar-da-ak-ki	a man unto thee.
še-ir-bi-i ù ú-ku-ul-tu	Send me for $\frac{1}{6}$th of a shekel of
ša $\frac{1}{6}$ šiqlu kaspim šu-bi-lim	silver, drink and food.
i-na an-ni-tim at-ḫu-ut-ki	May I therein recognize thy
lu-mur	sisterly disposition.

XXIX. (No. 62)

A request to return a run-away messenger and his brother to the writer.

A-na a-wi-lim	To the patrician,
qi- bi- ma	speak:—
um-ma A-wi-il-^{il}E-a-ma	Thus says Awîl-Ea:

[2] *ištu ilam tarši* literally translated means: thou hast since acquired a god. The phrase contains an idiomatic expression, which is not quite clear. The above rendering is only tentative. The "protecting genius" may have reference to Elmeshum's husband.

[3] *šu-ta-bi-li-im* mistake of scribe for *tu-ša-bi-li-im.*

[4] *iḫ-zu-ki* = "he took thee" in the sense of "he married thee." This is very common in Old Babylonian.

[5] With *^{is}a-am-ri-e* compare *amaru (iṣu)*, part of a bed; K 164:11; Craig, RT 78:1; 78:19 (here plural); Maḳlu V:2.

^{il}Šamaš ù ^{il}Marduk li-ba-al-li-ṭu-ka	May Shamash and Marduk keep thee well!
lu ša-al-ma-ta lu ba-al-ṭa-ta	Mayest thou be well and of good health.
ilu na-ṣi-ir-ka ri-eš-ka a-na da-mi-iq-tim	May the god who protects thee,
li- ki- il	uphold thy head for prosperity!
a-na šu-ul-mi-ka aš-pu-ra-am	I have written to greet thee.
šu-lum-ka ma-ḫar ^{il}Šamaš ù ^{il}Marduk	May thy well-being before Shamash
lu da- ri	and Marduk endure!
^{m}Sin-ra-bi lu redu ša bi-ti-ia	Sin-rabi, the messenger of my
ḫa-li-iq-ma	house has disappeared.
[a-na] A-wi-la-tum a-ḫi-šu	It is said: "they returned him
[i-na ....]kar-lik-ku	and gave him
[i-tu-]ur-šu-ma	to Awîlatum, his brother,
id-di-in-šu	in ......*karlikku.*
it-ta-la-ak-ma	He departed and
wa-ša-ab-šu i-na ali^{ki}	his stay is in the city,
ma-aḫ-ri-ka iq-bu-nim	in thy presence.
ki-ma ra-bu-ti-ka	Kindly
^{m}Sin-ra-bi	deliver over
ù A-wi-la-tum a-ḫi-šu	Sin-rabi and Awîlatum,
a-na ar-du ù id?-da-tum	his brother,
pi-qi-id-ma	to the servant and ......, and let
ma-aḫ-ri-ia li-iz-za-ni-iq?-šu-nu-ti	him arrive with them in my presence.

XXX. (No. 63)

Contains a demand for restitution of a stone tablet, an announcement of a retaliatory measure, and an inquiry into a certain action of the addressee.

A-na Sin-na-da	To Sin-nada,
qi- bi- ma	speak:—
um-ma Li-bi-it-ma	Thus says Libit:
^{il}Šamaš ù ^{il}Sin aš-šum-ia li-ba-al-li-ṭu-ki	May Shamash and Sin for my sake keep thee healthy!
ki-ma(?) šum-ma la ka-a-ti	As if there had been no explanation
pa-ri-is wa-ar-ka-tim	to thee about the matter!
la i-šu-ú ú-ul ti-di-e	Thou knowest not.

i-na ša-at-tim an-ni-tim	Render satisfaction unto me
ti-ri-in-ni-i-ma	this year and
na-ra-am šu-bi-ri-in-ni	hand over the stone tablet to me.
ṣi-ba-a-ti a-na pa-ni-ia	The things seized
ib-ši-i-ma	belong to me.
la a-ḫa-aš	I am in no haste
10 ma-na ri-iš[1] ^{m}*Gi-mil-la-at-Sin*	that Gimillat-Sin shall give thee
i-na-ad-di-ig-gi	the 10 mines of maintenance money.
aš-šum A-bil-^{il}*Ba-ú*	Concerning Abil-Bau,
ša-šu-ú ša i-ka-lu	him who is locked up,
ki-ta ma-la ba-aq-qu-ur-ki[2]	as much as there is truth to it,
ša ša-a-ti la tu-wa-aš-ša-ri-šu	having brought legal action against thee, because thou dost not let him
a-na ṣi-ir Sin-i-qu-lam[3]	go free, I took
al-qi-i-ma	to Sin-iqulam.
a-na Ud-bal-nam-ḫe	Let them bring thee
li-di-iḫ-ḫi-ki-i-ma	to Udbalnamḫe,
Šag. Warad li-iš-ku-na-ak-ki	and a servant let them provide for thee.
a-nu-um-ma ^{m}*Ú-tul-Ištar*	I, now, despatch unto thee
aṭ-ṭar-da-ak-ki-im	Utul-Ishtar.
ṭe-e-im ga-am-ra-am	Send
šu-up-ri	complete information.

XXXI. (No. 1)

A letter informing the addressee what he is to reply to another man's inquiry concerning a present. The second part of the letter entreats the recipient to give special attention to a person who has set his mind on something that is not proper.

A-na ^{il}*Sin-ma-gir*	To Sin-mâgir
qi- bi- ma	speak!
um-ma Ib-ku-Ištar ù Sin-i-tu-ra-am-ma	Thus say Ibku-Ishtar and Sin-itûram

[1] *Ri-iš*; compare Arabic *rîš* = "Fülle des Unterhaltes, Nahrung," here perhaps "maintenance, sustenance (money)."

[2] Mistake for: *buqqurki?*

[3] See note on this name in List of Personal Names.

aḫ- ḫu- ka- a- ma	thy brother:—
^{il}*Il-Aširta* ^{il}*Šamaš* ^{il}*Gál-gál-la ù* ^{il}*Amurru il-ka*	Il-Ashirta, Shamash, Galgalla and Amurru, thy
aš-šum-i-ni a-na da-ri-a-tim	god, for our sake grant
li- ba- al- li- ṭu- ú- ka	thee life forever!
^{m}*Ḫa-di-a-me-ir-*^{il} *amaš-ma aš-šum ni-di-in-tu-im*[1]	Ḫadiamer-Shamash (tells thee) as follows: "Concerning a present,
a-na ša-ni-im ir-šu-ú	which they have acquired for another (person)
ú-za-ab-ba-la-an-ni	they shall send (it) to me.
a-na i-ta-az-zu-uz-zi a-na ša-ši-im	In order to be portioned out to him
a-aḫ-ka la-a ta-na-an-di	be not negligent (in the matter)."
di-a-am qi-bi-šum um-ma at-ta-a-ma	Tell him the following information:
ša at-ta ga-ba eš-ma	"I have heard the word which
ta-ga-ab-bu-ú	thou sayest.
ia-ši-im we-iš-ṭum	Trouble is to me (because)
um-ma ga-bu-um-ma i-na ta-ak-lu-ú	the following is the word: "(It is) trustworthy,
^{m}*Ḫa-di-a-me-ir-*^{il}*Šamaš i-na te-ir-tim*	oh Ḫadiamer-Shamash, by that (same) order
iz-ba-tu-nim-šu	they have seized it (already)."
mi-nam ta-mu-ra-an-ni-ma	What dost thou see in me?
i-na ri-zi-nu um-ma	In our . . . . (thou hast said) as follows:
te-ir-ti a-na ša-ni-im	"Thou hast given my order to
ta-ad-di-in	another (person)".
ki-a-am qi-bi-šum-ma	Tell him thus and
ar-ḫi-iš i-ip-pa-al-ka	he will immediately answer thee.
ù a-nu-um-ma ^{m}*Na-bi-i-li-šu*	And now, Nabi-ilishu
a-na la-a-ši[2] *na-ṭi pa-nu-šu ša-ak-nu-ú*	has set his mind on what is not proper.
^{m}*A-bil-Sin a-wi-lam iš-da*[3]*-ma-am*	He has drugged Abil-Sin, the patrician.
i-na bi-it ^{il}*Sin i-na-az-za-aḫ*	He removes from the temple of Sin
šum-ma na-du-ú qi-bi-šum-ma	if he is negligent. Tell him that he must

[1] The writer by mistake first wrote the accusative ending *tam*, then he corrected it by adding simply *im* (*aššum nidintim.*)

[2] *la-a-ši* contracted from: *la-a i-ši.*

[3] Mistake of scribe for: *ištamam.*

ša aṣ-ṣi-im um la-a i-za-aḫ-ḫu-ur[4]
ù ki-ma ^{m}*A-bil-Sin nišakkam*[5]
ú-ul ti-di-e
a-na an-ni-tim a-aḫ-ka
la-a ta-na-an-di
^{il}*Il-Aširta* ^{il}*Šamaš* ^{il}*Gál-gál-la ù* ^{il}*Amurru il-ka*
aš-šum-i-ni a-na da-ri-a-tim
li-ba-al-li-ṭu-ú-ka

go out if he does not change.
Furthermore, because thou dost not know Abil-Sin,
the priest of sacrifice,
be not negligent in regard
to this (person).
May Il-Ashirta, Shamash, Galgalla and Amurru, thy god,
for our sake
grant thee life forever!

XXXII. (No. 45)

Concerning a wedding-gift and a present for the parental home.

A-na I-din-n[am]
qi- bi- [ma]
um-ma ^{il}*Sin-[X-ma]*
a-na bît a-wi-[lim]
a-li-ik-[ma]
1 biltam ša 30 [ma-na šipati piṣati]
ù 30 ma-na šipati šaplati
a-na bitim$^{(tim)}$ *li-qi-a-am-ma*
30 ma-na šipati pisati
a-na kallati aqarti
i-di-in
30 ma-na šipati šaplati
a-na bît ab-ba li-ši-ri-im-ma
i-na ku-nu-uk-ki-[šu]
li-ik-nu-uk-[su]

To Idinnam
say as follows:
Thus says Sin-X:—
Go to the house
of the patrician
and take away for me from
the house one load of 30
minas of white wool and 30
minas of lower grade wool.
Give to the highly esteemed
bride the thirty minas of
white wool.
Into the parental home
introduce the thirty minas of
lower grade wool. Let him seal
it with his seal.

XXXIII. (No. 32)

A royal request that the moon-god shall be taken away from a city, and that, moreover, a war prisoner shall be redeemed.

A-na Lu-uš-ta-mar-^{il}*Za-mà-mà*
ù Be-la-nu-um

To Lushtamar-Zamama
and Belanum

[4] סחר; for: *izaḫḫar*.

[5] Observe the uncommon ideographic writing: *NU.Ú.AB*.

qi- bi- ma	speak:—
um-ma Ḫa-am-mu-ra-bi-ma	Thus says Hammurabi:—
išten ^{il}*Sin a-na DUG.GAR*^{ki} *li-ṣu-ú*	Let them take forth from DUG.GAR one Sin (statue?).
I-ma-ni-nu-um	For Imaninum
ša na-ak-rum il-qu-ú[1]	whom the enemy has captured
10 mana kaspim i-na bît Sin	give ten minas of silver out
a-na tamqari-šu id-na-a-ma	of the temple of Sin to his merchant
pu-uṭ-ra-šu	and redeem him.

[1] We should expect: *ša* ...... *ilqû-šu.*

Notes.

The redemption price here mentioned is exorbitantly high, compared for instance with prices paid for slaves. According to Schwenzner's Tabelle 8 (Altbabylonisches Wirtschaftsleben, p. 110) the highest price paid, so far as attested up to the present, for a male slave is 90 shekels, i. e. 1½ mine (CT. VI. 29); the lowest price registered is 6 shekels (VS IX. 154).

§ 32 of the Code of Hammurabi refers to a case, which equals this one, where a ransom is to be paid for either a *redu* or a *ba'iru,* who might be captured while in the service of the king. According to this paragraph in the Code it seems to have been customary to place the money matter connected with the ransom into the hands of merchants. If the person to be ransomed was rich, he had to ransom himself, otherwise the obligation for paying the ransom price fell unto the temple of the city of which the ransomed had the right of a native. ("*šumma ina bitišu ša paṭarišu la ibašši ina bît ili ališu ippaṭṭar*", Col. XI. 25–29). The reference in our text to the temple of Sin indicates that, as the ransom price was so excessive, the temple-administration in conformity with a law equal to § 32 was obliged to redeem him. That the crown, however, took an interest in Imaninum shows him to be a person of some importance, perhaps a general of the royal army, or the like. This high station in life of Imaninum would explain the large amount asked for his redemption.

NAME LISTS.

A. Personal Names.

Attû: A-at-tu-ú; 148:1
Abâ: A-ba-a; 36:3
Aba-raḫam: A-ba-ra-ḫa-am; 15:13
Abi-^{il}Amurrum: A-bi-^{il}MAR.TU; 15:21
Abi-asât: A-bi-a-sa-at; 90:3
Abil-^{il}Adad: A-bil-^{il}IM; 41:7; 141:3
Abil-^{il}Amurrum: A-bil-^{il}MAR.TU; 95:2; 138:10
Abil-^{il}Baú: A-bil-^{il}Ba-ú; 63:16
Abil-ilu: A-bil-AN; 82:6; 82:16; 82:18
Abiljatum: A-bil-ja-tum; 102:4
Abil-Sin: A-bil-EN.ZU; 1:29; 1:33
Abil-^{il}Šamaš: A-bil-^{il}UD; 2:1; 35:3; 79:1; 143:1
Abum-waqar: A-bu-(um)-wa-qar; 39:1; 86:3; 123:6; 148:3; s. of *Warad-Sin:* 148:9; 148:17; 149:1; 149:13
Adâ: A-da-a; 41:1
^{il}Adad-êriš: ^{il}IM-PIN; 131:1
^{il}Adad-nâṣir: ^{il}IM-na-ṣir; 103:36
^{il}Adad-ra. . . ., ^{il}IM-ra-. . . .; 30:1
^{il}Adad-rîm-ili: ^{il}IM-ri-im-i-li; 87:3; 150:6
^{il}Adad-šar-ili: ^{il}IM-šar-i-li; 64:6
^{il}Adad-šarrum: ^{il}IM-šar-rum; 92:2
Aḫum-Aia: A-ḫu-um-A-a; 73:3
Aḫum-waqar: A-ḫu-(um)-wa-qar; 2:1; 89:7; 89:17; 124:1; 129:12
Aḫuni: A-ḫu-ni; 124:3
Aḫušina: A-ḫu-ši-na; 98:13
Âlik-idi: A-li-ik-i-di; 42:20
^{il}Amurrum-ibnišu: ^{il}MAR.TU-ib-ni-šu; 131:14
Ali-lûmur: A-li-lu-mu-ur; 95:1
^{il}Anu-mubaliṭ: ^{il}A-nu-mu-ba-li-iṭ; 18:1; 60:1
Arium-waqar: A-ri-um-wa-qar;[1] 143:1
Awat-^{il}Nannar: Awat-^{il}ŠEŠ^{ki}; 100:1
Awêl-^{il}Nabium: Awêl-^{il}Na-bi-um; 111:4
Awêl-^{il}Nannar: Awêl-^{il}ŠEŠ^{ki}; 83:3
Awîl-^{il}Adad: A-wi-il-^{il}IM; 35:1; 113:2
Awîlatum: A-wi-la-tum; 62:13; 62:22
Awîl-^{il}Ea: A-wi-il-^{il}E-a; 62:3
Awîlija: A-wi-li-ja; 71:1
Awîl-ili: A-wi-il-AN (i-li); 29:1; 78:7; 128:11; 140:3
Awîl-Ištar: A-wi-il-Ištar; 48:21; 48:24; 95:3
Awîl-^{il}Nabium: A-wi-il-^{il}Na-bi-um; 57:3; 68:3
Atanaḫ-ili: A-ta-na-aḫ-i-li; 103:32
Attija: At-ti-ja; 106:1
Babâ: Ba-ba-a; 81:1
Bakkum: Ba-ak-kum; 13:7
Bala: Bal-a; 7:1
Balmenamḫi: Bal-me-nam-ḫi; 96:1
Balmunamḫe: Bal-mu-nam-ḫe; 13:2; 77:4

[1] *A-ri-um-wa-qar* may simply be a mistake of the scribe for *A-ḫu-um-wa-qar.*

Baš-ilu: Ba-aš-AN; 107:1

Bêlanum: Be-la-nu-um; 32:2; 123:1

Bêlijašu: Be-li-ja-šu; 102:8

Bêlšunu: Be-el-šu-nu; 20:1; 28:1; 51:1; 58:1; 66:1; 85:1; 99:1; 103:1; 137:1; 142:1

Bêltani: Be-el-ta-ni; 53:7; 53:10; 53:17

Bêlî: Be-li-i; 26:1; 150:1

Bêlitia: Be-li-ti-ia; 16:1

Bili. . . : Bi-li-. . . ; s. of *Ili-ippalza:* 131: seal

Biliam: Bi-li-a-am; 64:9

Bilitum: Bi-li-tum; 129:6

Dadâ: Da-da-a; 17:1; 55:2; 112:1; 134:1

Dadaba: Da-da-ba; 101:3

Damqi-ilišu: Dam-qi-i-li-šu; 82:12

Dân-ilu: Da-an-AN; 139:1

Dapinum: Da-pi-nu-um; 33:3

Ea-ṣulul-šu: E-a-AN.DUL.-šu; 18:2; 60:3

Ea-gâmil: E-a-ga-mil; 108:1

Ea-nâṣir: E-a-na-ṣi-ir; 49:21

Ea-šarram: E-a-šar-ra-am; 39:11

Ea-ṣili: E-a-ṣi-li; 77:2

Êku-Urra: E-ku-Ur-ra; 138:1

Elmešum: El-me(š)-šum; 15:1; 144:11

Elmeštum: El-meš-tum; 117:3

Erara: E-ra-ra; 9:13

Eriri: E-ri-ri; 44:1

Êribam: E-ri-ba-am; 40:13; 40:16

Êribam-Sin: Eri-ba-am-Sin; 132:3

Etel-pî-^{il}Marduk: E-tel-KA-^{il}AMAR. UD; 120:3

Etel-pî-^{il}Nabium: E-tel-KA-^{il}Na-bi-um; 71:3

Gatiluma: Ga-ti-i-lu-ma; 24:3

Gimillum: Gi-mi(l)-lum, Gi-mi-el-lum; 22-3; 92:7; 110:7

Gimillat-Sin: Gi-mil-la-at-XXX; 63:14

Ḫabil-aḫi: Ḫa-bil-a-ḫi; 125:4

Ḫadi-amêr-^{il}Šamaš: Ḫa-di-a-me-ir^{il}UD; 1:9; 1:19

Ḫammurabi: Ḫa-am-mu-ra-bi; 19:30; 32:4

^{il}Ḫani-mušalim: ^{il}Ḫa-ni-mu-ša-lim; 47:9

Ḫâziram (Acc.): *Ḫa-zi-ra-am;* 74:5

Ḫâzirum: Ḫa-zi-ru-um; 135:3

Ḫununi: Ḫu-nu-ni; 147:9

Ibija: I-bi-ja; 73:1

Ibi-^{il}Ilabrat: I-bi-^{il}NIN.ŠUBUR; 38:5; 78:17

Ibi-Sin: I-bi-EN.ZU; 19:1

Ibi-^{il}Šamaš: I-bi-^{il}UD; 70:5; 132:1

Ibiq-nâr-kimḫi: Šig-Îd-kim-ḫi; 106:3

Ibku-Ištar: Ib-ku-Ištar; 1:3; 69:1

Ibkuša: Ib-ku-ša; 2:4; 143:3

Ibni-^{il}Adad: Ib-ni-^{il}IM; 68:1

Ibni-Ea: Ib-ni-E-a; br. of *Ilušu-ibni* and s. of *Idin-. . . . ;* 38:8; 38:21

Idin-. . . . : I-din-. . . . ; f. of *Ilušu-ibni* and *Ibni-Ea:* 38:9

Idin-^{il}Adad: I-din-^{il}IM; 93:3

Idin-Ea: I-din-E-a; 88:1

Idinjatum: I-din-ja-tum; 13:10; 13:12

Idin-^{il}Amurrum: I-din-^{il}MAR.TU; 145:6; 145:14

Idin-E.MAḪ (?): I-din-E.MAḪ (EN?); 33:10

Idin-EN.MUN: I-din-EN.MUN; 36:5

Idinnam: I-din-nam; 45:1; 102:5

Idin-^{il}Nanâ: I-din-^{il}Na-na-a; 48:23; 103:27; 131:5

Idin-Sin: I-din-EN.ZU; 50:20; 136:3

Idin-Urra: I-din-Ur-ra; 116:1; 121:1; 128:1

Igmatum: Ig-ma-tum; s. of *Sin-gâmil;* 130:14

Igmil-Sin: Ig-mil-EN.ZU; 13:6; 19:19; 37:1

Ili-abi: I-li-a-bi; 146:10

Ili-aḫta: I-li-aḫ-ta; 108:7

Ili-gimlanni: I-li-gim-la-an-ni; 87:5; 87:8

Ili-idinnam: I-li-i-din-nam; 8:6; 41:17; 146:3

Ilijatum: I-li-ja-tum; 96:4

Ili-ippalzam: I-li-ip-pa-al-za-am; 26:3; 41:15; 69:3; 117:18; 135:1

Ili-iqîšam: I-li-i-qi-ša-am; 64:20; 70:3; 126:4

Ilima-abi: I-li-ma-a-bi; 37:20

Ili-mutîr: I-li-LAḪ; 77:1

Ili-rabi: I-li-ra-bi; 12:3

Ili-šarram: I-li-šar-ra-am; 49:4

Ilu-abia: AN-a-bi-ia; 141:1

Ilu-da-.....: AN-da-.....; 57:1

Iluma-ilê: AN-ma-i-li-e; 17:3

Ilušu-bâni: AN-šu-ba-ni; 54:2

Ilušu-ibni: AN-šu-ib-ni; 110:5

Ilušu-ibišu: AN-šu-i-bi-šu; s. of *Warad-Sin:* 25:5; 25:13; 38:15; 83:5

Ilušu-ibnišu: AN-šu-ib-ni-šu; 10:3; 75:3

Ilušu-nâṣir: AN-šu-na-ṣi-ir; 107:3

Iltani: Il-ta-ni; 61:3

Imaninum: I-ma-ni-nu-um; 32:6

Imgur-^{il}Dagan: Im-gur-^{il}Da-gan; 138:3

Immun-^{il}Marduk: Im(?)-mu-un(?)-^{il}AMAR.UD; 20:9

Inbi-ilišu: In-bi-i-li-šu; 40:1

Inbi-^{il}Sin: In-bi-^{il}EN.ZU; 139:1

Ini-^{il}Ea: I-ni-^{il}E-a; 101:5; 101:20

Ini-^{il}Sin: I-ni-^{il}EN.ZU; 47:1

Iranum: Ir-an-um (or *Sanum?*)*;* 152:3

Irṣia: Ir-ṣi-ia; 53:1

Ištâ: Iš-ta-a; 147:1

^{il}Ištar-šumu: ^{il}Ištar-šu-mu; 26-10

Igurum: I-gu-rum; 34:14

Jaḫzir-ilu: Ja-aḫ-zi-ir-AN; 96:5

Kamnia: Ka-am-ni-ia; 79:3

KA-ša-Ištar: KA-ša-Ištar; 152:1

KA-ša-Urra: KA-ša-Ur-ra; 24:1

^{il}KAŠ.AM.GAR.RA...?; 88:6

Ku.........; 104:1

Kubbutia: Ku-ub-bu-ti-ia; 7:3

Kulira...: Ku-li-ra-...; 80:1

Kunna: Ku-un-na; 31:1

Kurdi-Ištar: Kur-di-Ištar; 66:3

Lalatum: La-la-tum; 100:3

Lalutum: La-lu-tum; 48:1

Libit: Li-bi-it; 63:3; 114:6

Libit-Ea: Li-bi-it-E-a; 33:15

Liku-^{il}: Li-ku-^{il}; 96:3

Libur-šadûni: Li-bur-ša-du-ni; 54:4

Litûr-Sin: Li-tu-ur-EN.ZU; 2:6

Lûmur-ša-^{il}Marduk: Lu-mur-ša-^{il}AMAR.UD; 3:3; 81:6; 109:26

Luštamar-Sin: Lu-uš-ta-mar-EN.ZU; 103:28

Luštamar-^{il}Zamàmà: Lu-uš-ta-mar-^{il}Za-mà-mà; 32:1

Mattatum: Ma-at-ta-tum; 25:6; 25:11; 25:15; 25:19

Majari: Ma-ja-ri; 98:9; 98:12; 98:16

Manum: Ma-a-nu-um; 72-8; 72:9

Mannum-kîma-^{il}Adad: Ma-an-nu-um-ki-ma-^{il}IM; 11:31; 125:5

Sin-êriš: EN.ZU-PIN; 19:1; 67:13; 72:3; 88:3

Sin-galdu: EN.ZU-gal-du; 80:3

Sin-gâmil: EN.ZU-ga-mil; f. of *Igmatum:* 130:14

Sin-i.....: EN.ZU-i-.....; 136:1

Sin-idinnam: EN.ZU-i-din-nam; 6:1; 19:18; 43:3; 68:8; 74:3; 78:12; 82:2

Sin-ilišu: EN.ZU-i-li-šu; 38:27

Sin-iqîšam: EN.ZU-i-qi-ša-am; 23:1; 40:9; 56:1; 74:1; 91:1

Sin-iqulam: EN.ZU-i-ku-lam;[1] 63:20

Sin-ilu: EN.ZU-AN; 86:16

Sin-išmeanni: EN.ZU-iš-me-(a)-(an)-ni; 64:1; 150:8

Sin-imguranni: EN.ZU-im-gur-an-ni; 47:3; 82:23

Sin-ippalzam: EN.ZU-ip-pa-al-za-am; 133:9

Sin-itûram: EN.ZU-i-tu-ra-am; 1:3

Sin-itašu: EN.ZU-i-ta-šu; 151:3

Sin-li.....: EN.ZU-li-....; 12:1

Sin-lîrik: EN.ZU-li-ri-ik; 95:7

Sin-mâgir: EN.ZU-ma-gir; 1:1; 4:3; 27:9; 102:7; 110:5; 116:3; 116:5; 121:3; 128:3

Sin-mâlik: EN.ZU-ma-lik; 9:12; 29:14

ilSin-manse: ilEN.ZU-ma-an-se; 118:3

Sin-ma-ilu: EN.ZU-ma-AN; 108:3

Sin-muballiṭ: EN.ZU-mu-ba-al-li-iṭ; 33:6

Sin-mušalim: EN.ZU-mu-ša-lim; 67:1; 150:2

Sin-muštal: EN.ZU-mu-uš-ta-al; 10:5; 34:2

Sin-nada: EN.ZU-na-da; 63:1

Sin-natum: EN.ZU-na-tum; 31:5

Sin-wedu: EN.ZU-we-du; 19:41

Sin-rabi: EN.ZU-ra-bi; 62:11; 62:21

(il)Sin-rîmeni: (il)EN.ZU-ri-me-ni; 86:1; 86:9; 131:3

Sin-šamuḫ: EN.ZU-ša-mu-uḫ; 92:1; 97:3; 107:8; 120:1

Sin-šarrum: EN.ZU-šar-rum; 102:3

Sin-tâiar: EN.ZU-ta-a-a-ar; 37:2

Sin-tiûm: EN.ZU-ti-u-um; 40:15

Sin-úzili: EN.ZU-ú-zi-li; 55:1; 112:2; 112:10; 112:41; 134:2

Sirum: Si-ru-um; 15:3

Sizî: Si-zi-i; 106:1

Ṣili-.....: Ṣi-li-.........; 22:1

Ṣili-ilAdad: Ṣi-li-ilIM; 113:4; 149:7

Ṣili-ilDamkina: Ṣi-li (Ṣili)-ilDam-ki-na; 54:1; 92:4

Ṣili-ilušu: Ṣi-li-AN-šu; 82:19

Ṣili-ilŠamaš: Ṣi-li-ilUD; 33:11; 49:3; 77:8; 94:3; 110:3

Ṣili-Urra: Ṣili-Ur-ra; 127:7

ilṢiru-qarrad: ilṢIR-qar-ra-ad; 39:3

ilŠamaš-..........; 49:19

ilŠamaš-dînam-îdi: ilUD-di-nam-i-di; 4:7

ilŠamaš-edû: ilUD-e?-du?-ú; 101:14

ilŠamaš-ḫâṣir: ilUD-ḫa-ṣi-ir; 9:11; 19:3; 20:3; 28:3; 51:3; 51:17; 58:3; 99:3; 103:2; 137:3; 142:3

ilŠamaš-igmil: ilUD-ig-mil; 37:4

[1] In *BE* Vol. VI, Part 2, No. 33, line 5 (Rev.) the same verbal element appears in the name I-li-i-qu-lam, which Poebel read Ili-ibašar = "Sin will loosen." The tablet as well as the case read plainly Ili-iqulam. The meaning probably is "my god (or in the above case, Sin) has paid attention to me."

B. List of Countries, Cities, Villages, Walls, Rivers and Canals.

C. Names of Gods.

Gula: ^{il}*Gu-la*
 PN: *Nabi-*^{il}*Gula*
Ḫamutam: ^{il}*Ḫamutam*
 PN: ^{il}*Ḫamutam*
Ḫani: ^{il}*Ḫa-ni*
 PN: ^{il}*Ḫani-mušalim*
Ilabrat: ^{il}*NIN.ŠUBUR*
 48:4; 132:4
 PN: *Ibi-*^{il}*Ilabrat*
Il-Ištar (or *Aširta*) = אל-עשׁתרת, אל־עסתור;
 1:5; 1:37
Ištar: *Ištar*, (^{il}*Ištar*)
 43:4
 PN: *Ištar-šumu; Awîl-, Ibku-, Kurdi-, Mâr-, Útul-Ištar*
Lugal-banda: ^{il}*Lugal-mar-da*
 138:4
Marduk: ^{il}*AMAR.UD*
 2:3; 6:4; 11:3; 14:4; 19:26; 25:4; 30:4; 31:4; 38:6; 42:3; 46:5; 52:3; 62:4; 62:9; 68:4; 70:4; 71:4; 78:3; 79:4; 81:4; 82:3; 97:4; 98:4; 105:4; 106:4; 109:4; 117:4; 119:4; 123:4; 125:3; 127:4; 139:4; 142:4; 144:3; 146:4; 148:4; 151:4
 PN: *Marduk-. . . . . . ., -bâni, -lamazašu, -muštal, -mušalim, -nâṣir, -raḫi. . .; Etelpî-, Lûmurša-, Riša-*^{il}*Marduk*
Nabium: ^{il}*Na-bi-um*
 38:2
 PN: *Nabium-mâlik; -waqar; Awîl-, Etel-pî-Nabium*
Nanâ: ^{il}*Na-na-a*
 PN: *Idin-*^{il}*Nanâ*
Nannar: ^{il}*ŠEŠ*^{ki}
 PN: *Awat-, Awêl-*^{il}*Nannar*
Nergal: ^{il}*NE.UNU.GAL*
 21:4; 39:4; 72:4; 114:4; 129:1; 150:3
Ningirsu: ^{il}*Nin-gir-su*
 126:5
Ningišzida: ^{il}*Nin-giš-zi-da*
 PN: ^{IL}*Ningišzida*
Ninuba. . . .: ^{il}*Ni-nu-ba-. . . .*
 61:4
Sin: *EN.ZU*, ^{il}*EN.ZU*, XXX
 32:5; 32:8; 52:13; 52:22; 52:28; 63:4; 103:35
 PN: *Sin-. . . . .; -aba, -abu-kullim, -abum, -aiabaš, -bêl-ili, -bilaḫ, -duršu, -êribam, -êriš, -galdu, -gâmil, -i. . . . ., -idinnam, -ilišu, -iqîšam, -iqulam, -ilu, -iš-meanni, -imguranni, -ippalzam, -itûram, -itašu, -li. . . . ., -lîrik, -mâgir, -mâlik, -manse, -mailu, -muballiṭ, -mušalim, -muštal, -nada, -natum, wedu, -rabi, -rîmeni, -šamuḫ, -šarrum, -tâiar, -tiūm, -úzili; Abil-, Êribam-, Ibi-, Igmil-, Litûr-, Luštamar-, Nabi-, Šeib-, Warad-Sin*
Šamaš: ^{il}*UD*
 1:5; 1:37; 2:3; 3:4; 5:4; 6:4; 7:4; 8:4; 9:4; 10:4; 11:3; 13:5; 14:4; 15:4; 17:4; 18:3; 19:4; 20:4; 21:4; 25:4; 26:4; 27:4; 28:4; 30:4; 31:4; 33:4; 34:3; 35:4; 36:4; 38:6; 39:4; 40:4; 41:4; 42:3; 46:5; 47:4; 48:4; 51:4; 52:3; 53:4;

LIST OF LETTERS.

Text No.	Addressed to	Sent by	Catalog YBC
1	*Sin-mâgir*	*Ibku-Ištar ù Sin-itûram*	4519
2	*Aḫum-waqar ù Abil-*^{il}*Šamaš*	*Warad-*^{il}*Šamaš*	5458
3	. . . . . . *ù*	*Lûmur-ša-*^{il}*Marduk*	5465
4	*Sin-êribam*	*Sin-mâgir*	5474
5	*Nûr-*^{il}*Šamaš*	*Sin-bêl-ablim*	6135
6	*Sin-idinnam*	^{il}*Marduk-mušalim*	4527
7	*Bala*	*Kubbutia*	4541
8	*Šunum-ilu*	*Šumum-libši*	4540
9	*Sin-îribam*	^{il}*Šamaš-mâgir*	6123
10	*Watar-*^{il}*Šamaš*	*Ilušu-ibnišu*	4559
11	*Nabi-*^{il}*Ša[maš]*	^{il}*Marduk-[nâṣir]*	4546
12	*Sin-li*	*Ili-râbi*	5459
13	*Nabi-*^{il}*Gula ù Balmunamḫe*	*Sin-aiabaš*	6129
14	*Na[bi-*^{il}*Šamaš]*	^{il}*Marduk-nâ[ṣir]*	7012
15	*Elmešum*	*Sirum*	4516
16	*Bêlitia*	*Sin-abum*	4523
17	*Dadâ*	*Iluma-ilie*	4564
18	^{il}*Anu-mubaliṭ*	*Ea-ṣulul-šu*	4579
19	*Sin-êriš ù Ibi-Sin*	^{il}*Šamaš-ḫâṣir*	5589
20	*Bêlšunu*	^{il}*Šamaš-ḫâṣir*	7062
21	*Bêlia*	*Urra-gâmil*	4505
22	*Ṣili-*	*Gim[illu]m*	5470
23	*Sin-iqîšam*	*Nûr-*^{il}*Adad*	4529
24	*KA-ša-Urra*	*Gati-iluma*	5461
25	*Muḫaddum*	*daianê*^{meš} *Bâbili*^{ki}	5463
26	*Bêlî*	*Ili-ippalzam*	4554
27	*Šumi-aḫia*	^{il}*Šamaš-mubaliṭ*	5460
28	*Bêlšunu*	^{il}*Šamaš-ḫâṣir*	4545
29	*Awîl-ilu*	^{il}*Šamaš-nâṣir*	5472
30	^{il}*Adad-ra*	*Ib-*	6127
31	*Kunna*	*Muḫuški*	4568
32	*Luštamar-*^{il}*Zamàmà ù Bêlanum*	*Ḫammurabi*	4521
33	. . . . *-ša?-na-Aia*	*Dapinum*	4569
34	*Watar-*^{il}*Šamaš*	*Sin-muštal*	4510
35	*Awîl-*^{il}*Adad*	*Abil-*^{il}*Šamaš*	4560
36	*Abia*	*Abâ*	4534
37	*Igmil-Sin ù Sin-tâiar*	^{il}*Šamaš-gâmil*	5592

Text No.	Addressed to	Sent by	Catalog YBC
38	*[Awî]lim*	*Ibi-*^{il}*Ilabrat*	4587
39	*Abum-waqar*	^{il}*Ṣiru-qarrad*	5591
40	*Inbi-ilišu*	*Watar-*^{il}*Šamaš*	4518
41	*Adâ*	*Šîb-*^{il}*Adad*	4508
42	*Šabiria*	*Taribatum*	4566
43	*Ziḫâ*	*Sin-idinnam*	4583
44	*Eriri*	*Nabi-*^{il}*Sin*	4507
45	*Idinnam*	*Sin-. . . . .*	4577
46	*Awilim*	^{il}*Marduk-bâni*	6119
47	*Ini-*^{il}*Sin*	^{il}*Sin-imguranni*	5588
48	*Lalutum*	*Šeib-Sin*	4562
49	*Bêlia*	*Ṣili-*^{il}*Šamaš*	6141
50	*Munawirum*	*Tišanatum*	6131
51	*Bêlšunu*	^{il}*Šamaš-ḫâṣir*	4550
52	*Bel[t]i*	*Munawirum*	7015
53	. . . . *ù Irzia*	*Nabi-*^{il}*Šamaš*	6998
54	*Ṣili-*^{il}*Damkina ù Ilušu-bâni*	*Libur-šadûni*	6124
55	*Sin-úzili*	*Dadâ*	7042
56	*Sin-iqîšam*	*Nûr-*^{il}*Adad*	4548
57	*Ilu-da. . . . . . .*	*Awil-*^{il}*Nabium*	5466
58	*Bêlšunu*	^{il}*Šamaš-ḫâṣir*	6126
59	*Bêlia*	*Samia*	5469
60	^{il}*Anu-mubaliṭ*	*Ea-ṣulul-šu*	6125
61	*Ummia*	*Iltani*	4501
62	*Awilim*	*Awil-*^{il}*Ea*	4572
63	*Sin-nada*	*Libit*	6133
64	*Sin-išmeanni*	*Sabitum*	4580
65	*Sin-iqîšam*	*Sin-rabi*	5467
66	*Bêlšunu*	*Kurdi-Ištar*	4514
67	*Sin-mušalim*	*Urra-išpiel*	4585
68	*Ibni-*^{il}*Adad*	*Awil-*^{il}*Na[bium]*	4563
69	*Ibku-Ištar*	*Ili-ippalzam*	4567
70	^{il}*Šamaš-liwir*	*Ili-iqîšam*	4515
71	*Awilia*	*Etel-pî-*^{il}*Nabium*	4556
72	*Abia*	*Sin-êriš*	4509
73	*Ibia*	*Aḫum-Aia*	4531
74	*Sin-iqîšam*	*Sin-idinnam*	4543
75	*Martu-*^{il}*Abâ*	*Ilušu-ibnišu*	4544
76	*Muḫaddum*	^{il}*Marduk-mušalim*	7022
77	*Ili-mutîr ù Ea-ṣili*	*Balmunamḫe*	5462
78	*Bêlia*	*Sin-gâmil*	5471
79	*Abil-*^{il}*Šamaš ù madûtim*	*Warad-*^{il}*Šamaš ù Kamnia*	7010
80	*Kulira. . . .*	*Sin-galdu*	4506
81	*Babâ*	*Munawirum*	5468
82	*Bêlia*	*Sin-idinnam*	4520

Text No.	Addressed to	Sent by	Catalog YBC
83	*Ûbarrum*	*Amêl-^{il}Nannar*	7060
84	*Zijatum*	*^{il}Šamaš-lamazašu*	4524
85	*Bêlšunu*	[*^{il}Samas-ḫâṣir*]	5050
86	*Sin-rîmeni ù Abu-waqar*	*^{il}Zamàmà-ilu*	6121
87	*Nabi-^{il}Šamaš*	*^{il}Adad-rîm-ili*	4542
88	[*I*]*din-Ea*	*Sin-êriš*	4512
89	*Ablum*	*Mâr-Larsa^{ki}*	4565
90	*Bêlia*	*Abi-asât*	4537
91	*Sin-*[*i*]*qîšam*	[*Nûr-^{il}Adad*]	4530
92	*Sin-šamuḫ ^{il}Adad-šarrum Šunatum Ṣili-^{il}Damkina ù madûtim*	*Gimillum*	6138
93	*Aḫia ù belia*	*Idin-^{il}Adad*	4552
94	*Bêlia*	*Ṣili-^{il}Šamaš*	6122
95	*Ani-lûmur Abil-^{il}Amurrum Awil-Ištar ù madûtim*	*Šarrum-kîma-ili ù Sin-lîrik*	6132
96	*Balmenamḫi*	*Liku-^{il}?*	4551
97	*Šabirini*	*Sin-šamuḫ ù madûtim*	4525
98	*^{il}Marduk-muš*[*tal*]	*^{il}Marduk-mušalim*	4513
99	*Bêlšunu*	*^{il}Šamaš-ḫâṣir*	4579
100	*Amât-^{il}Nannar*	*Lalatum*	6140
101	*Watar-^{il}Šamaš*	*Dadaba*	7011
102	*Munawirum*	*Sin-šarrum Abil-jatum ù Idinnam*	6139
103	*Bêlšunu*	*^{il}Šamaš-ḫâṣir*	6835
104	*Ku*.......	....	7008
105	*Šumi-aḫia*	*^{il}Nabium-mâlik*	4570
106	*Sizî ù Attia*	*Ibiq-nâr-kimḫi*	4581
107	*Bâš-ilu*	*Ilušu-nâṣir*	7063
108	*Ea-gâmil*	*Sin-mailu*	6128
109	*Akil^{meš} Amurrim, akil*...	*Rabianum ù šibut âlim^{ki}*	5590
110	*Bêlia*	*Ṣili-^{il}Šamaš*	4526
111	....	....	6120
112	*Dadâ ù ^{il}Sin-úzili*	*Šeib-^{il}Sin*	5489
113	*Nûr-^{il}Šamaš Awil-^{il}Adad Sin-bilaḫ Ṣili-^{il}Adad ù PA.NAM.Û.UD^{meš} (=madûtim?)*	*^{il}Šamaš-nâṣir*	4549
114	*Warad-^{il}Šamaš*	*Watar-^{il}Šamaš*	5464
115	....	*^{il}Šamaš-ma*.........	4528
116	*Idin-Urra*	*Sin-mâgir*	4533
117	*Awilim*	*Elmeštum*	4538
118	*Zijatum*	*^{il}Sin-manse*	4571
119	*Awilim*	*^{il}Marduk-nâṣir*	4558
120	*Sin-šamuḫ*	*Etel-pî-^{il}Marduk*	7061
121	*Idin-Urra*	*Sin-mâgir*	4532
122	.......*banu*	..........*zi*........	4535
123	*Bêlanum*	*Munawirum*	6137

Text No.	Addressed to	Sent by	Catalog YBC
124	*Aḫu-waqar*	*Aḫuni*	4557
125	*Nabi-ilŠamaš*	*ilMarduk-nâṣir*	4536
126	*Awilim*	*Ili-iqîšam*	4573
127	*Nabi-ilŠamaš*	*ilMarduk-nâṣir*	6130
128	*Idin-Urra*	*Sin-mâgir*	4575
129	*AB.AB.UL*	*Watar-ilŠamaš*	4561
130	*Šurim*		4553
131	*ilAdad-êriš*	*ilSin-rîmeni*	5473
132	*Ibi-ilŠamaš*	*Êribam-Sin*	4586
133	*Abia*	. . . .	4513
134	*Dadâ ù ilSin-úzili*	*Seib-ilSin*	4522
135	*Ili-ippalzam*	*Ḫâzirum (?)*	6833
136	*Sin-iqîšam*	*Idin-Sin*	6997
137	*Bêlšunu*	*ilŠamaš-ḫâṣir*	7014
138	*Êku-Urra*	*Imgur-ilDagan*	6999
139	*Dân-ilu ù Inbi-Sin*	*Sani*	4582
140	*Bêlia*	*Awil-ilu*	6136
141	*Ilu-abia*	*Abil-ilAdad*	4578
142	*Bêlšunu*	*ilŠamaš-ḫâṣir*	4574
143	*Arium-waqar ù Abil-ilŠamaš*	*Ibkuša*	4555
144	*Nabi-ilŠamaš*	*ilMarduk-nâṣir*	7013
145	*Pirḫum*		7016
146	*Zizia*	*Ili-idinnam*	7006
147	*Ištâ*	*Mâr-Ištar*	6836
148	*Âttû*	*Abu-waqar*	7002
149	*Abu-waqar*	*Aḫu-waqar*	7007
150	*Bilî*	*Sin-mušalim*	6134
151	*Šabiria*	*Sin-itašu*	7059
152	*KÀ-ša-Ištar*	*Iranum*	4504

AUTOGRAPHED TEXTS

1

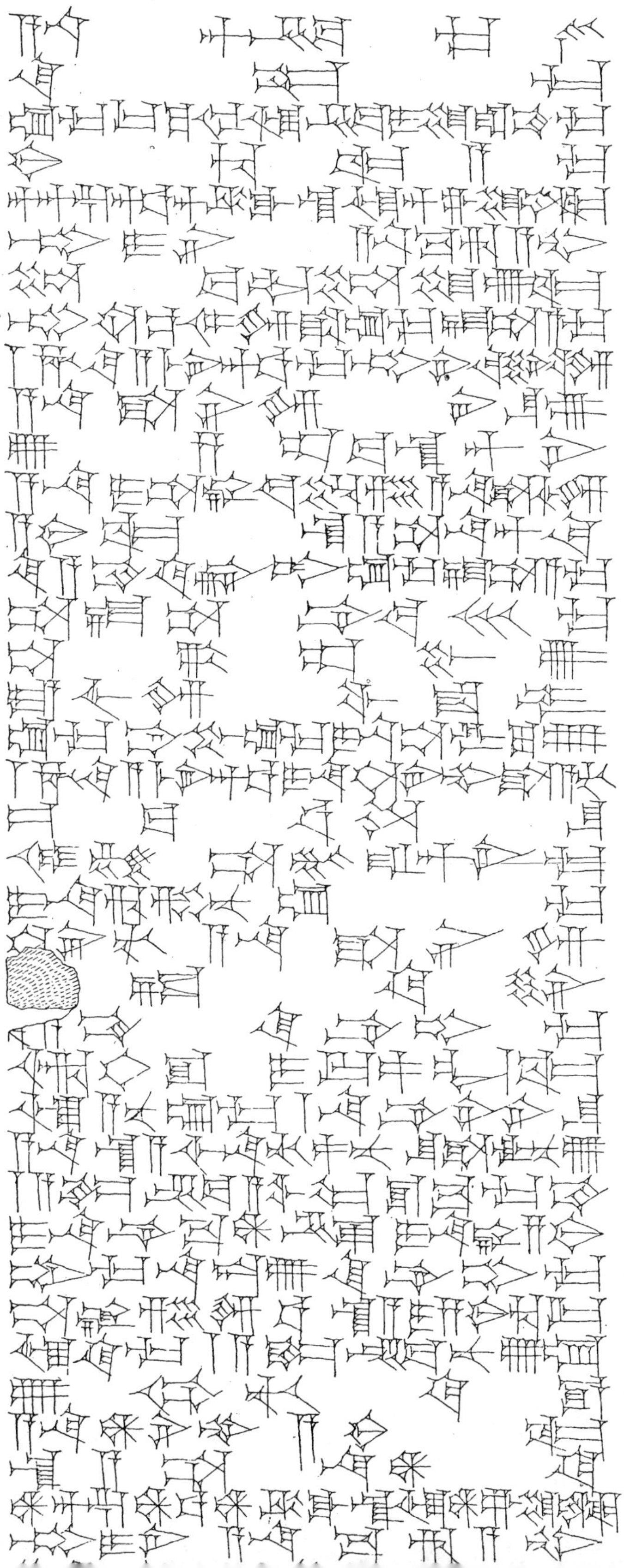

2

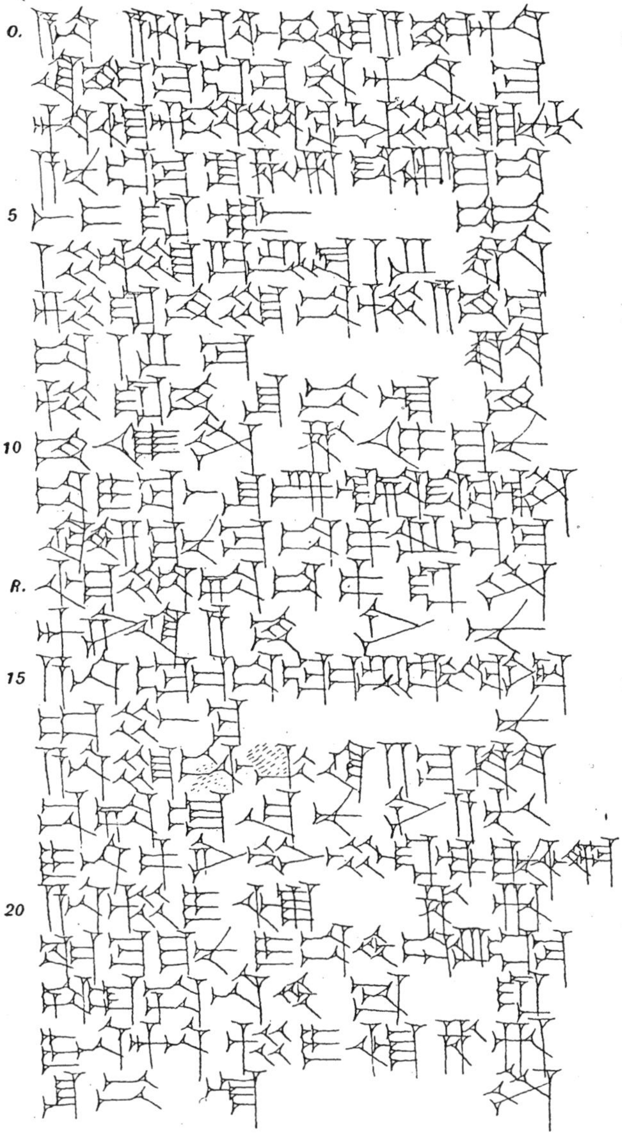

3

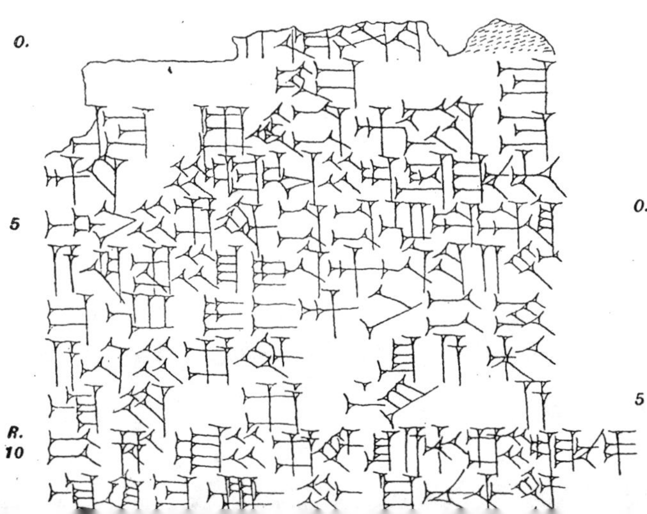

4

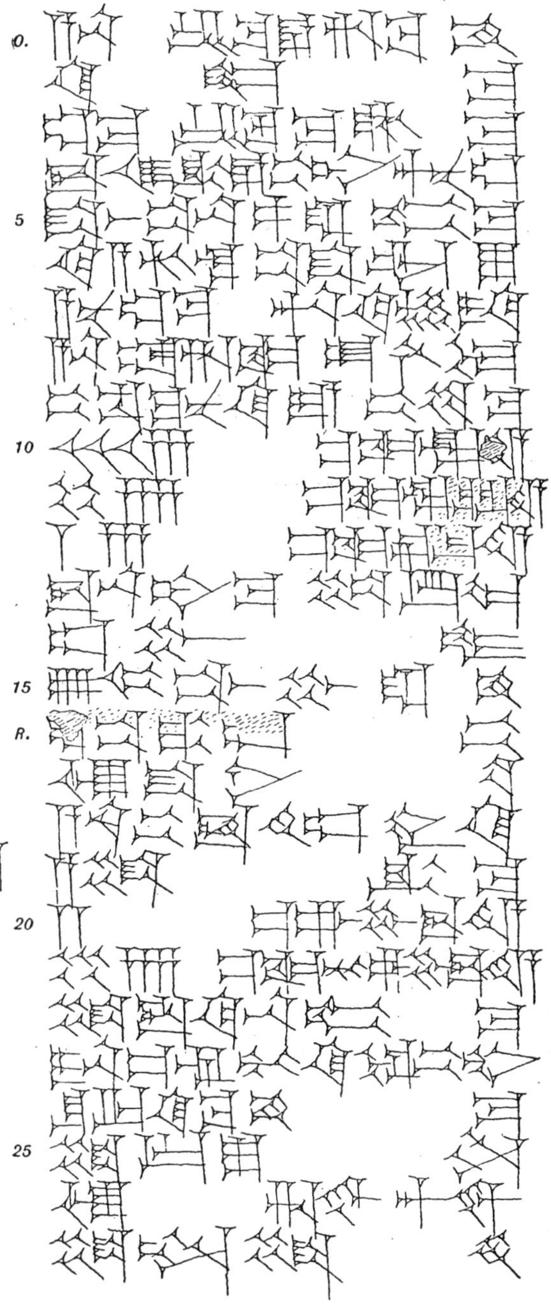

5

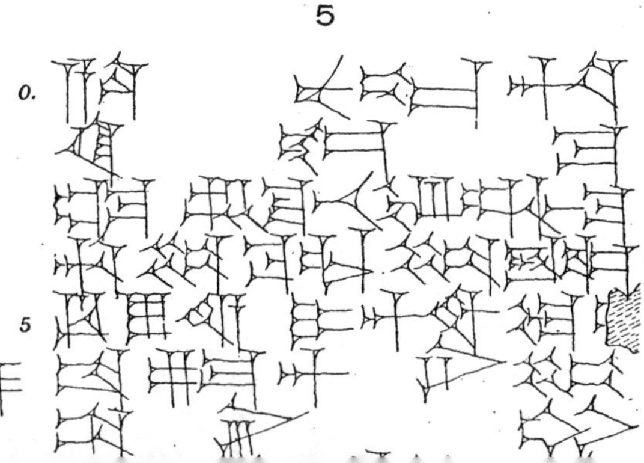

6

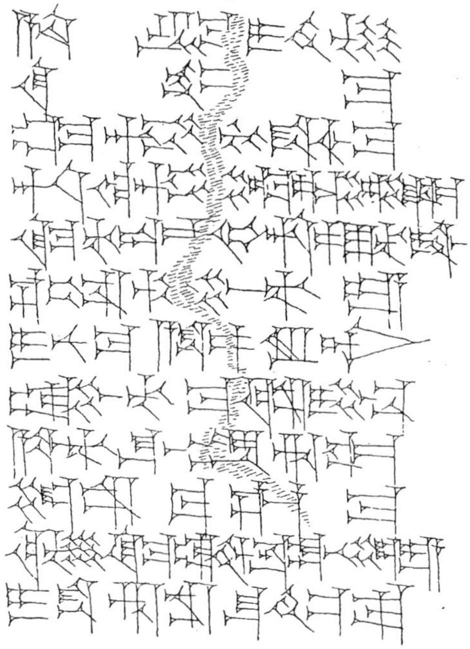

9

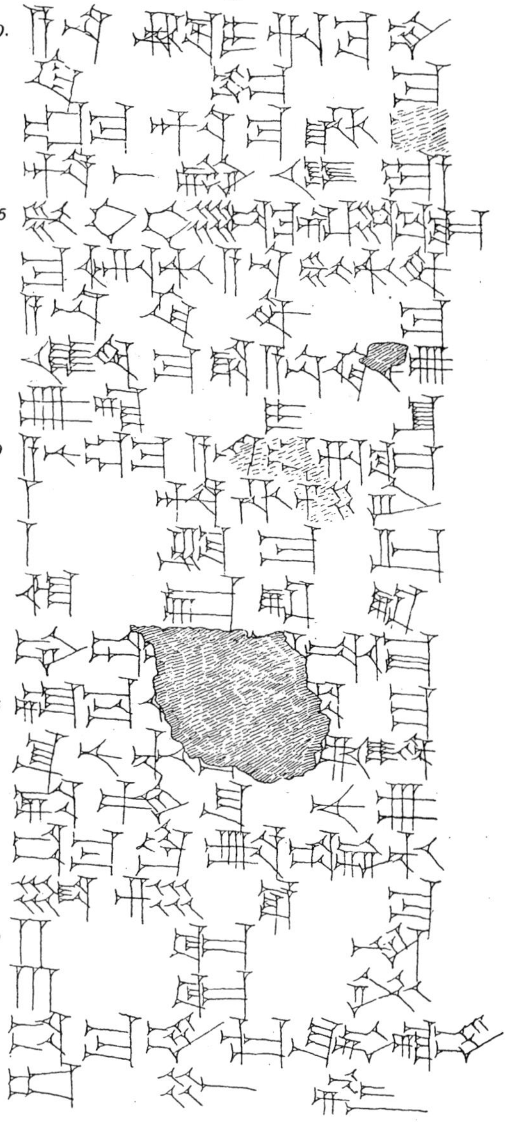

7

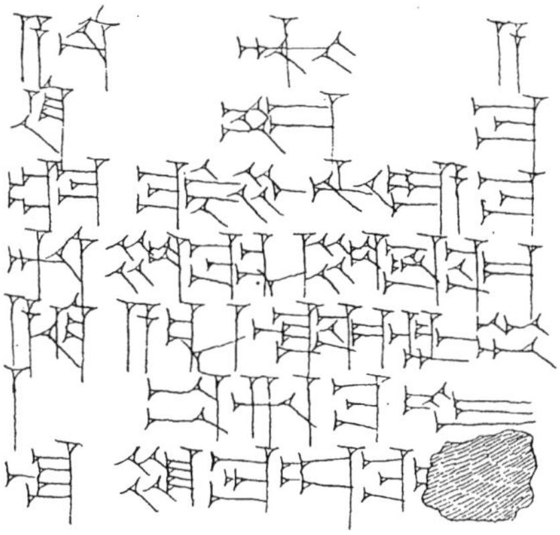

8

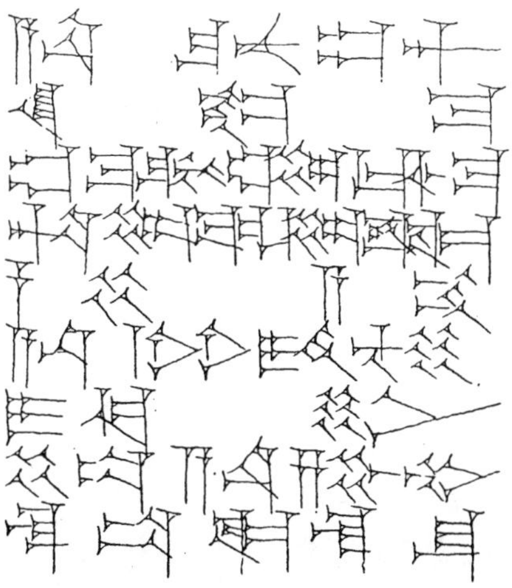

10

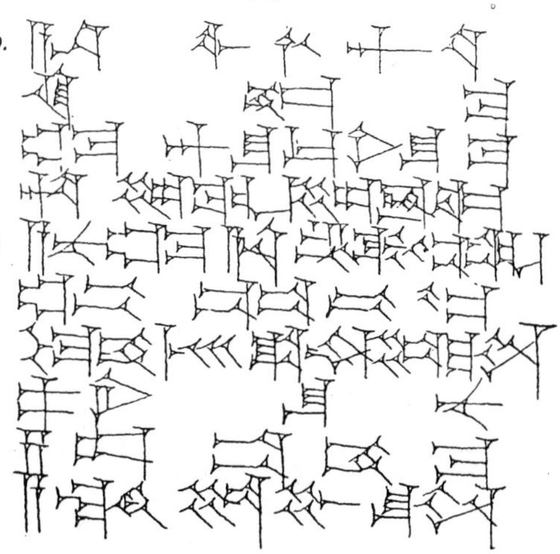

11

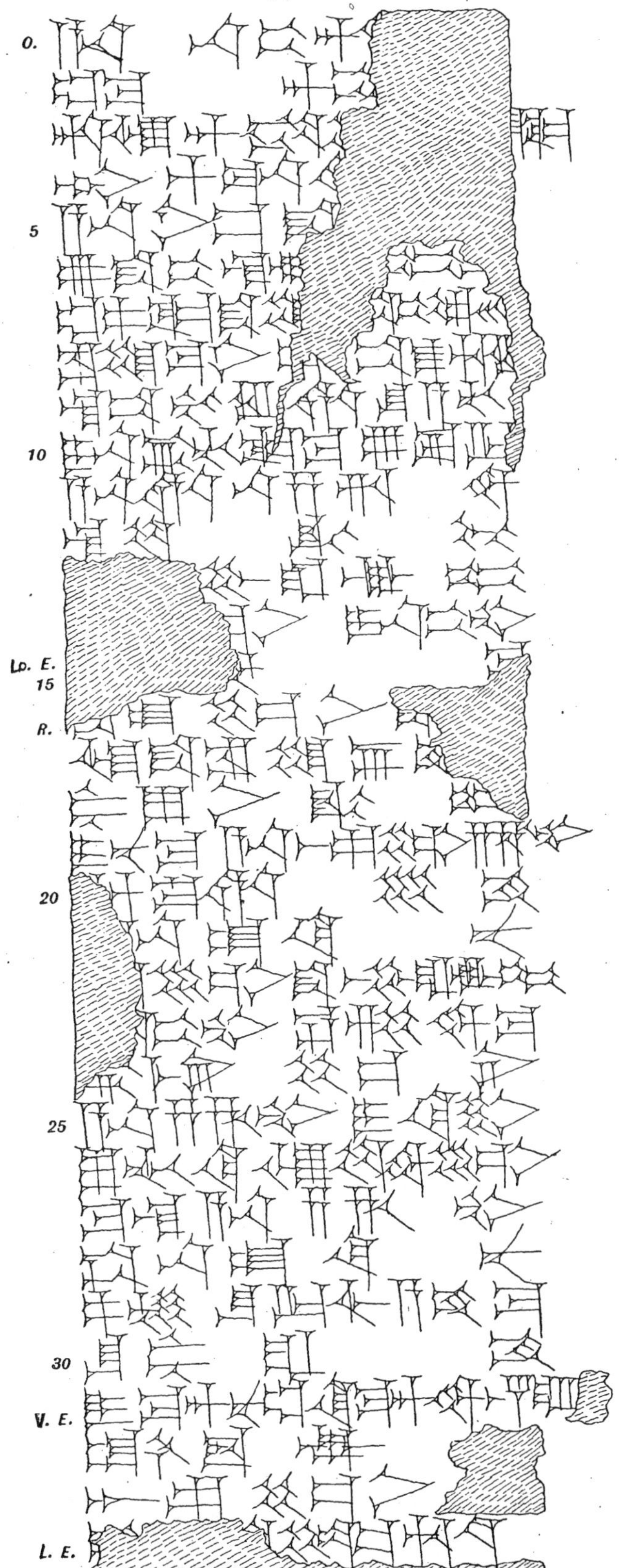

12

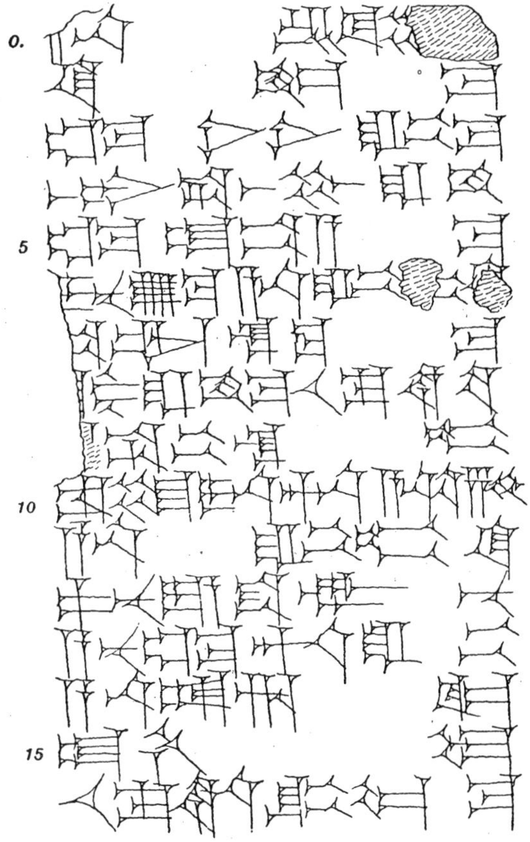

13

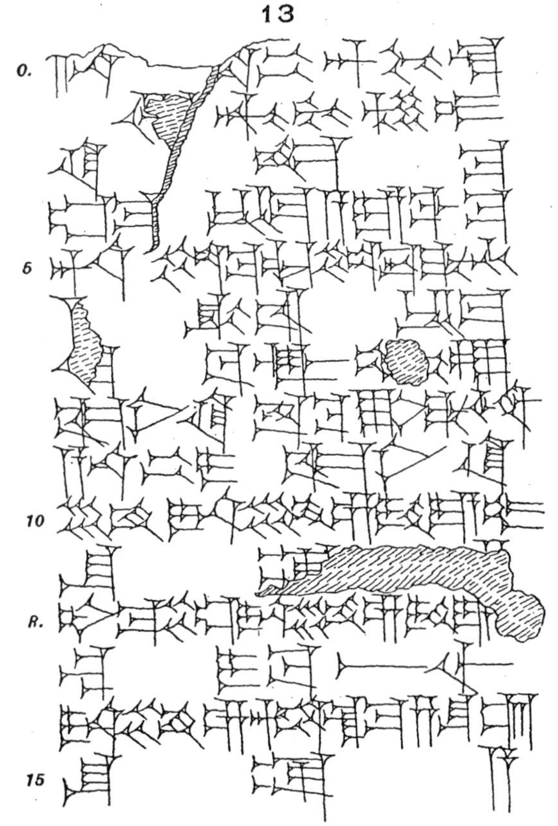

14

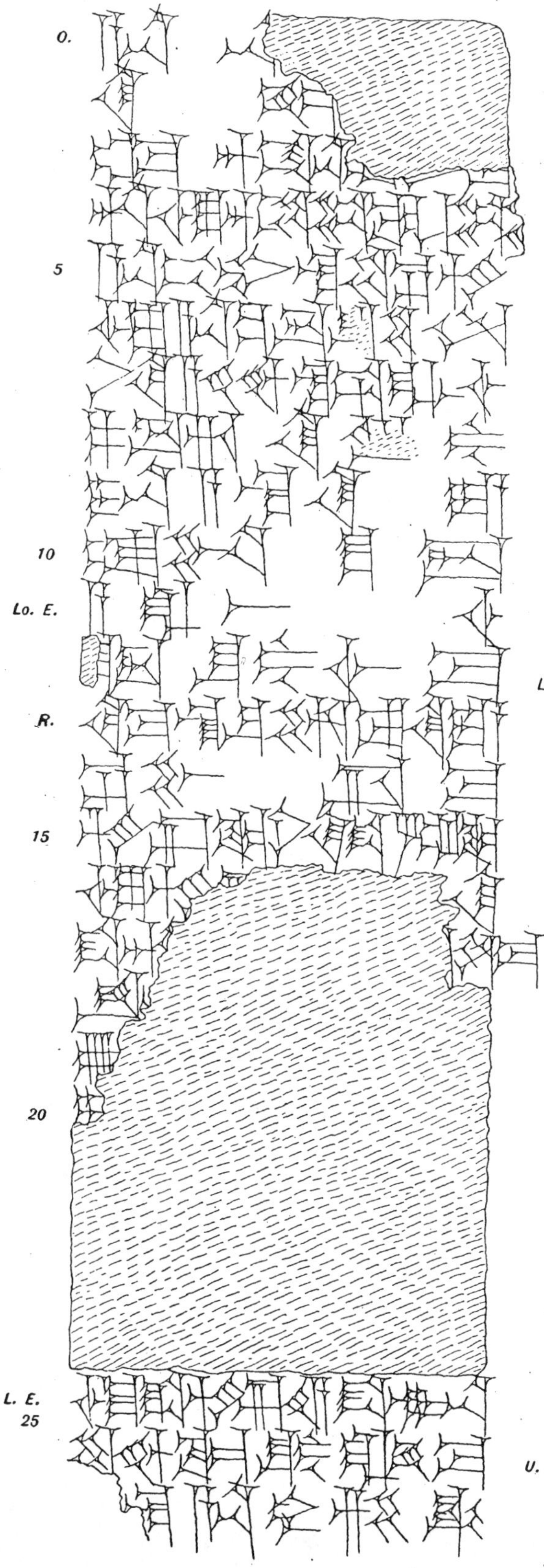

15

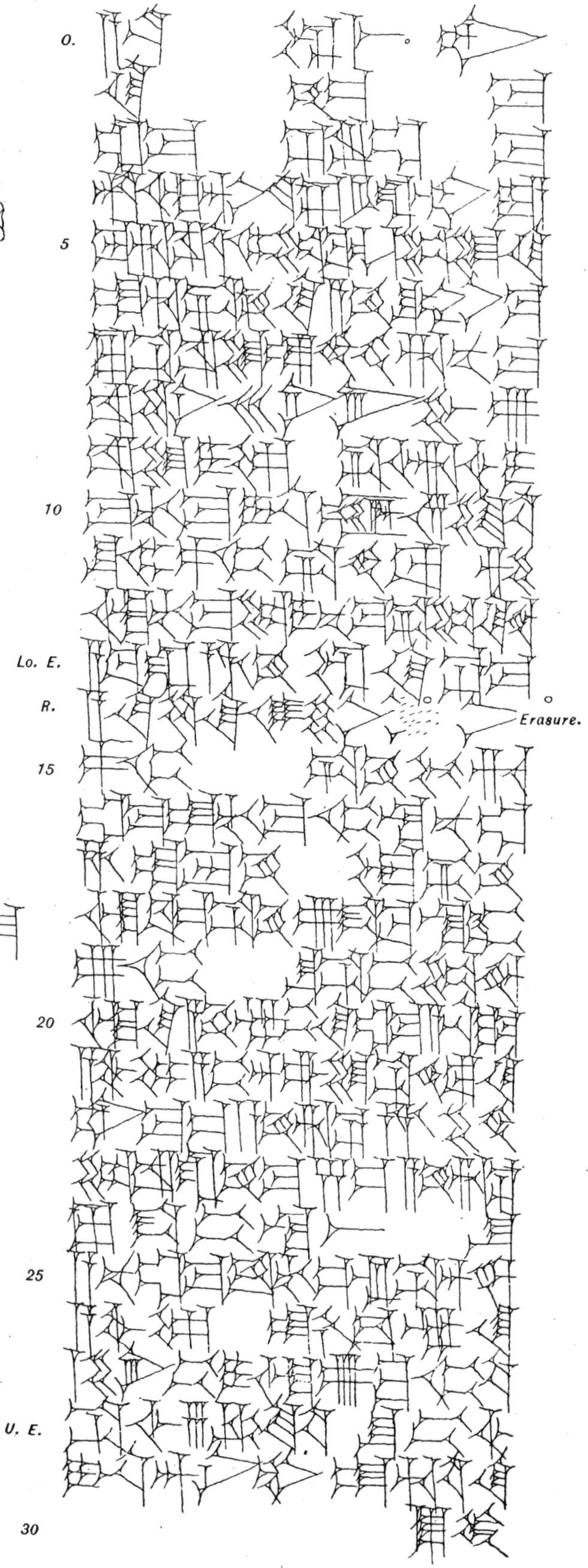

16

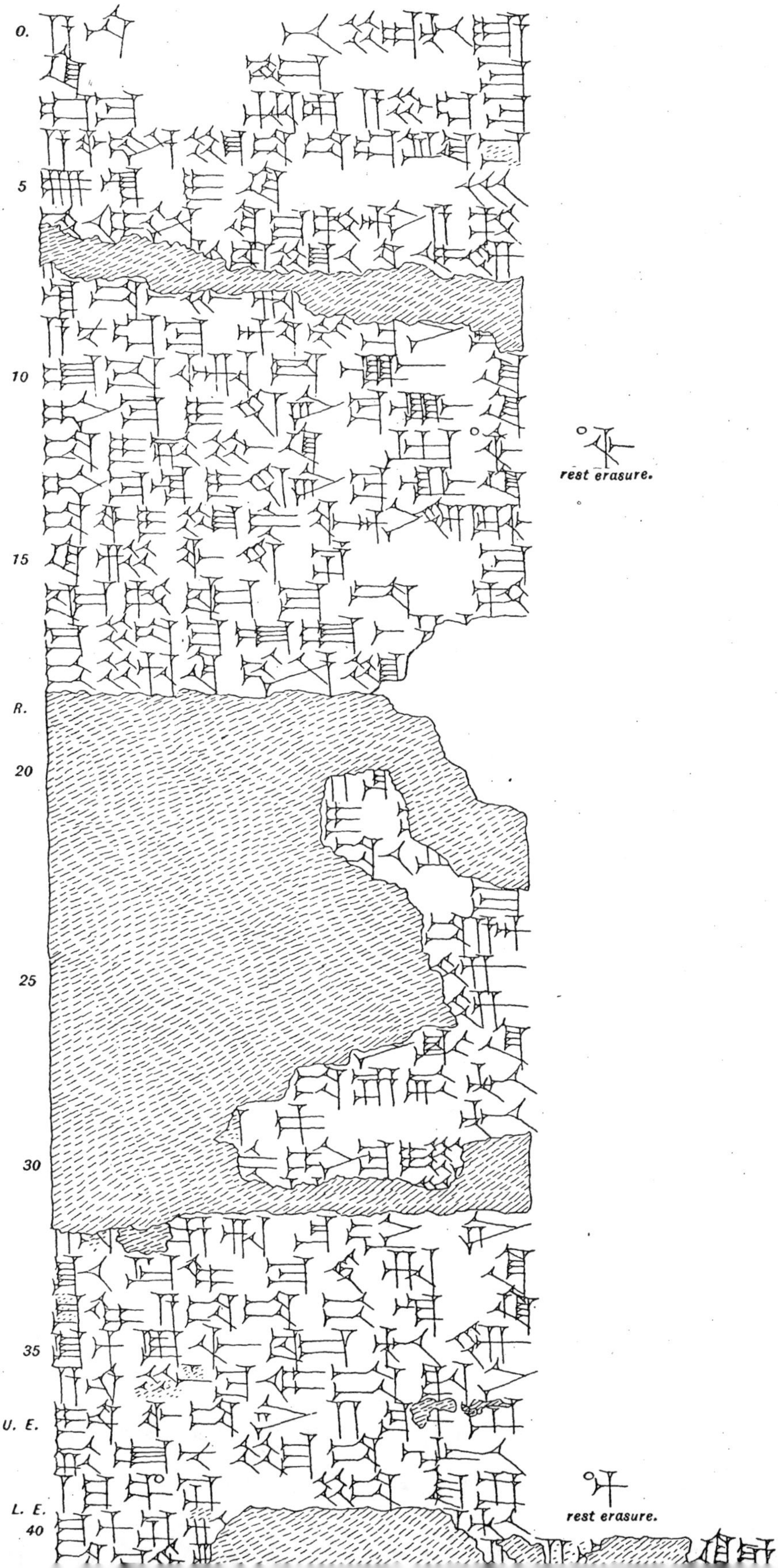

17

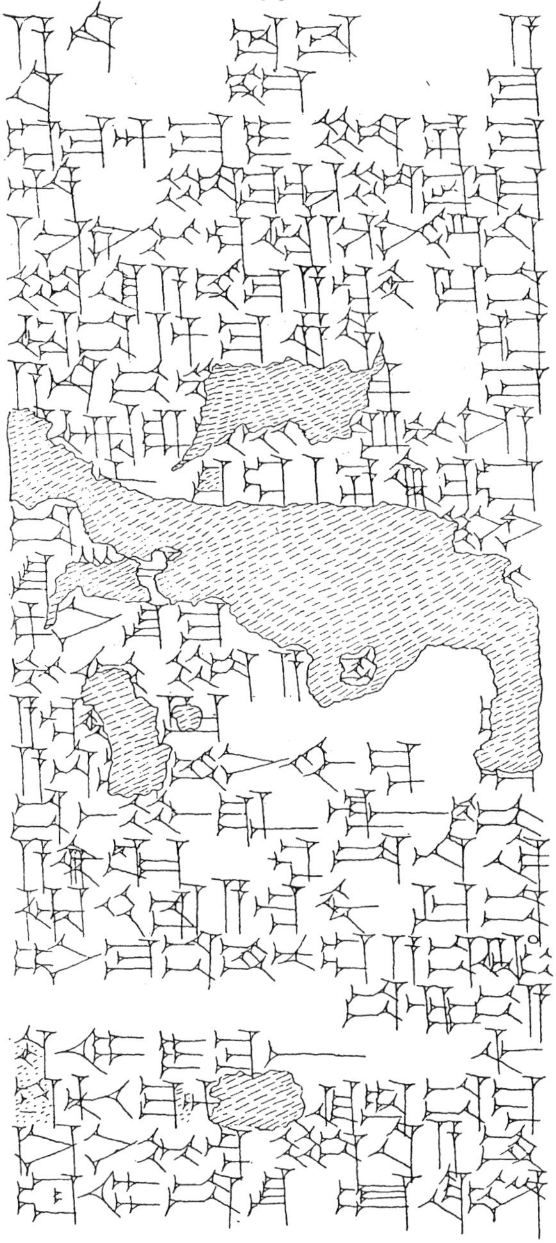

18

19

O.

Lo. E.

R.

U. E.

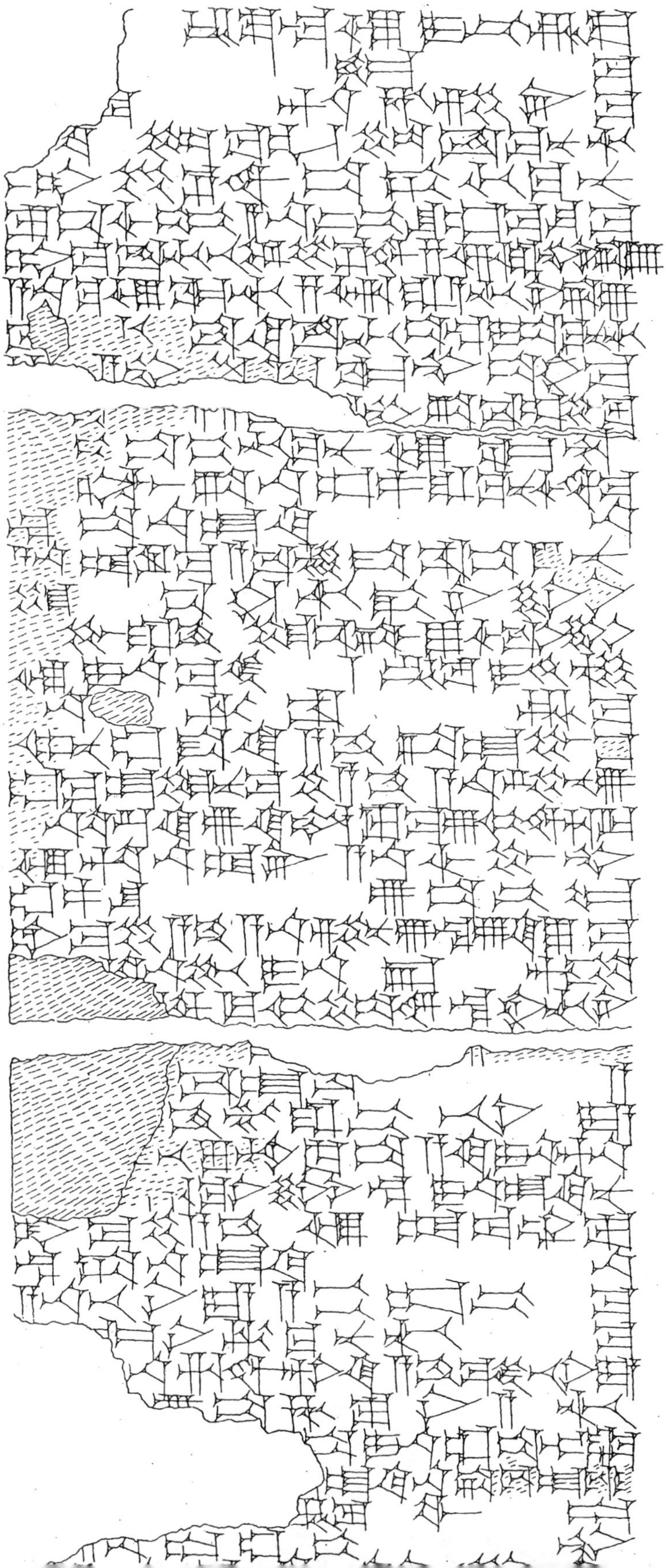

20

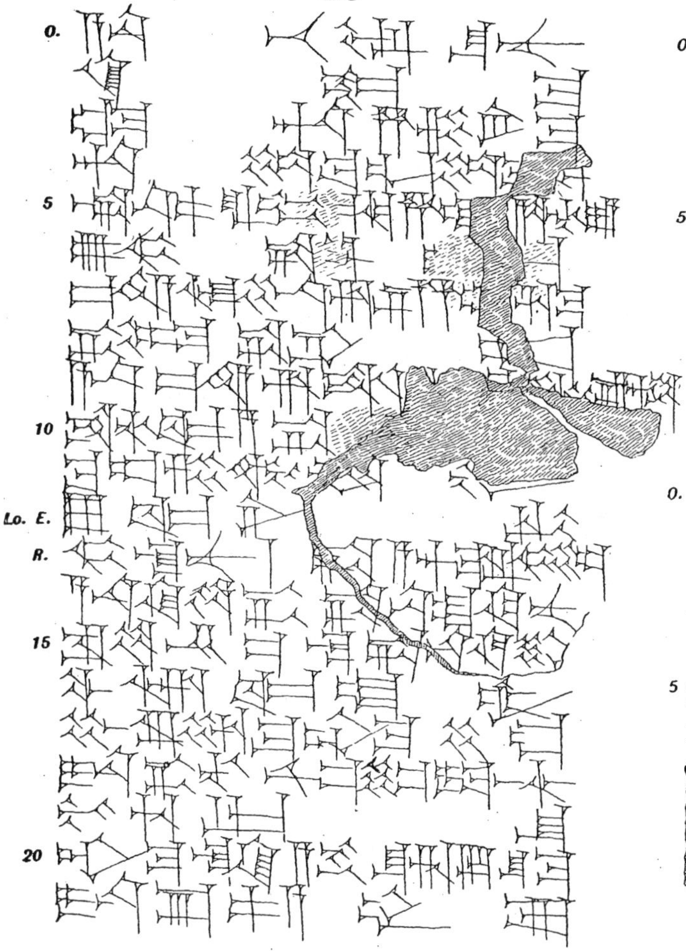

22

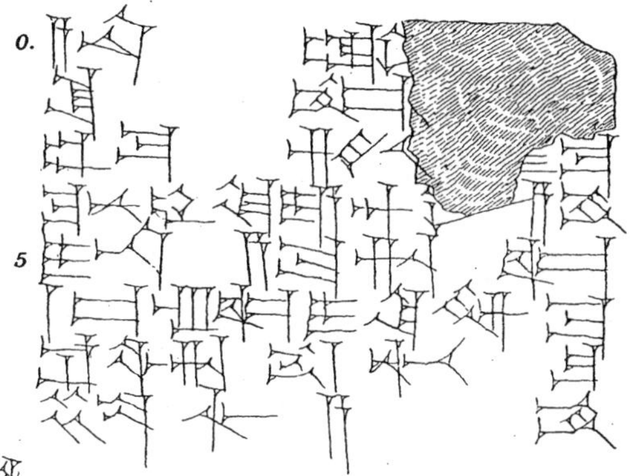

23

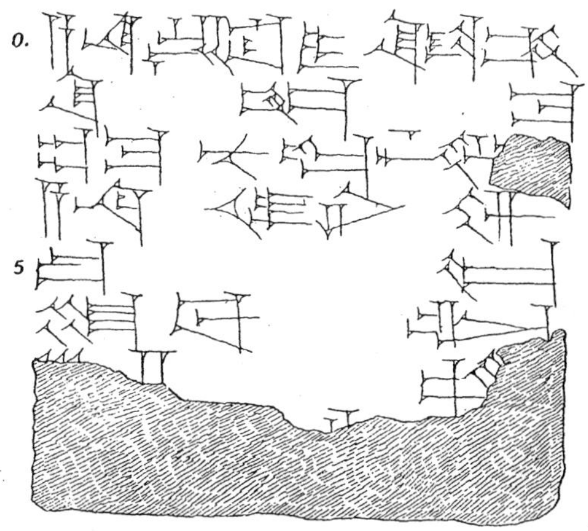

21

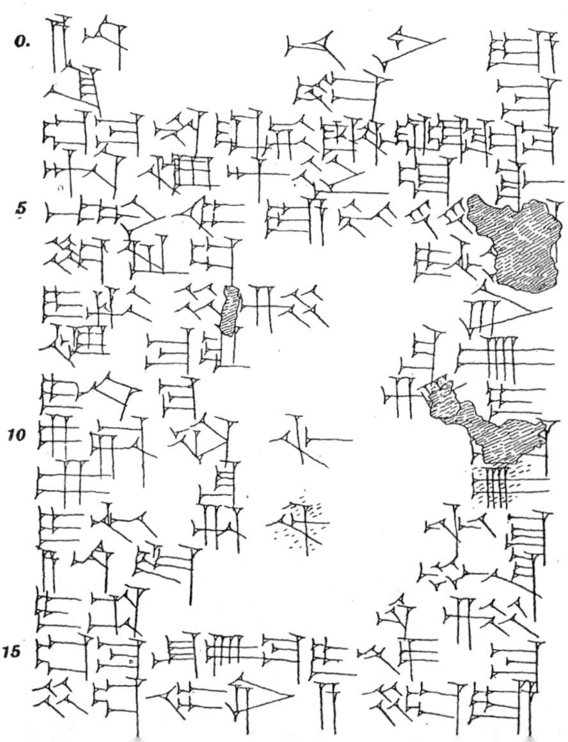

24

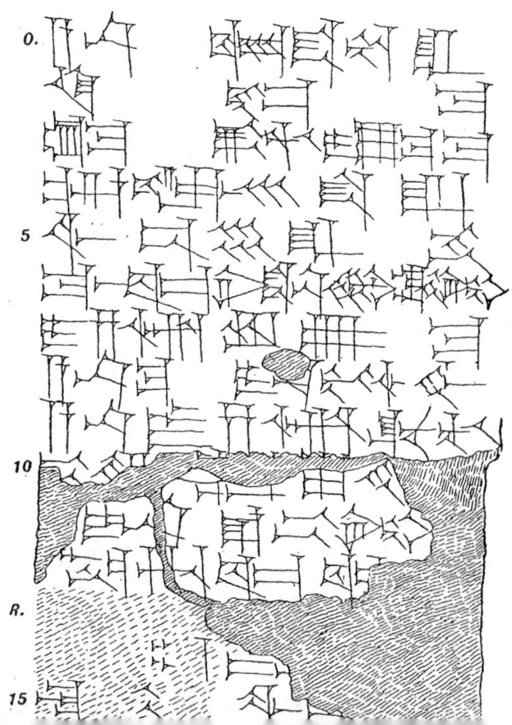

25

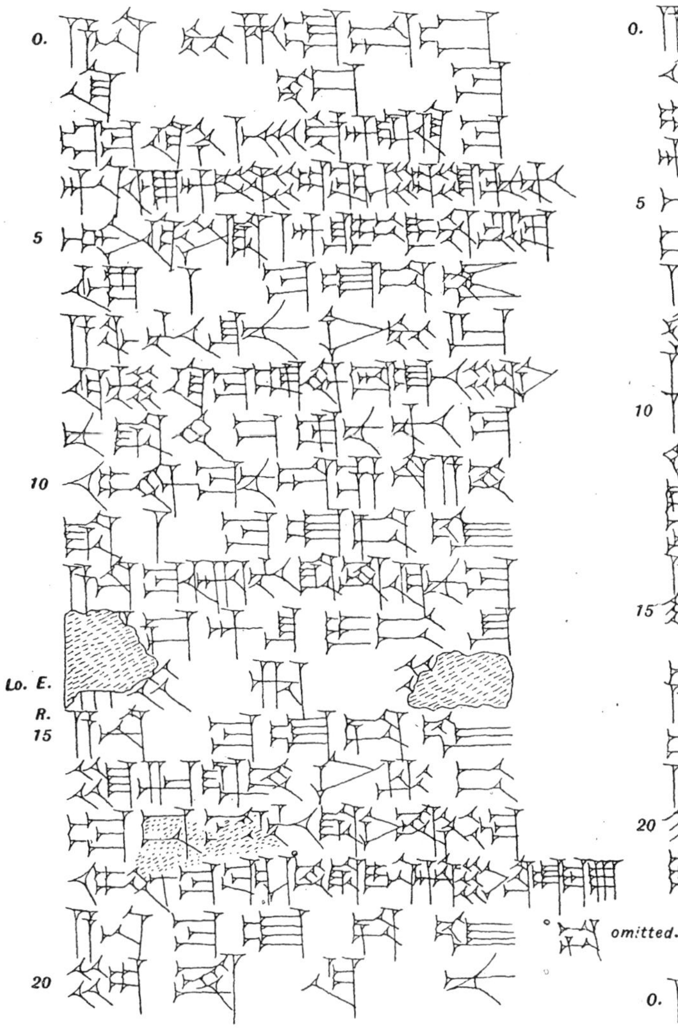

26

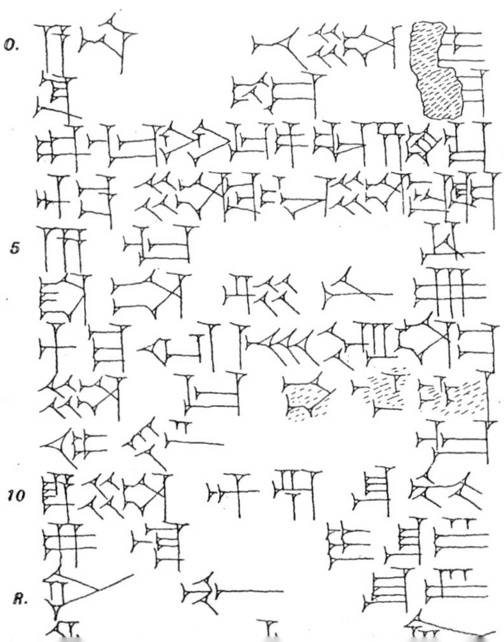

27

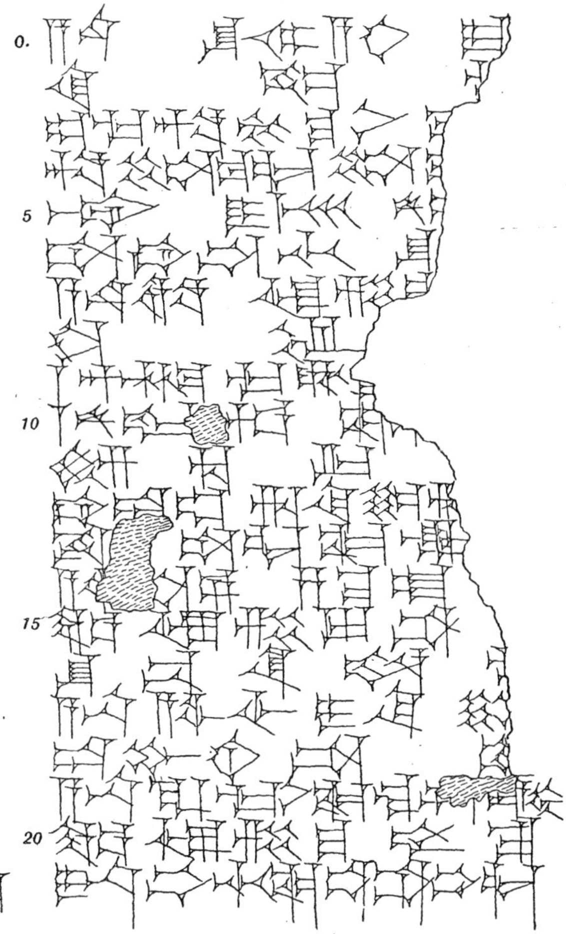

28

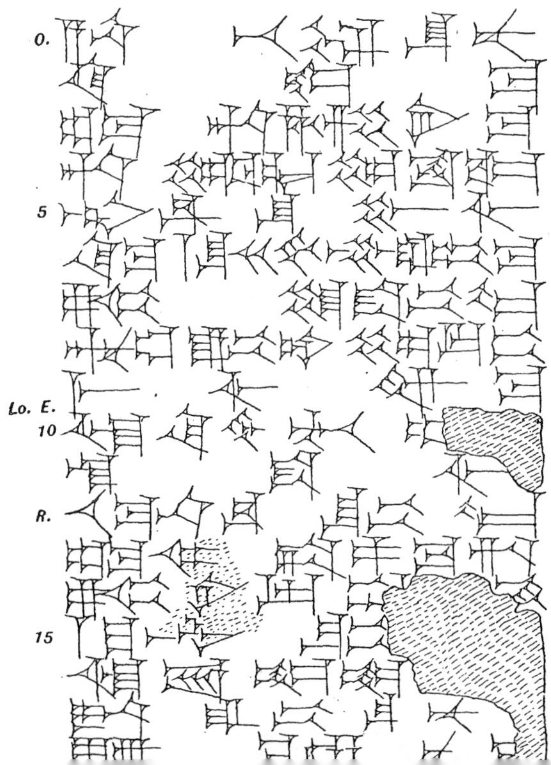

29

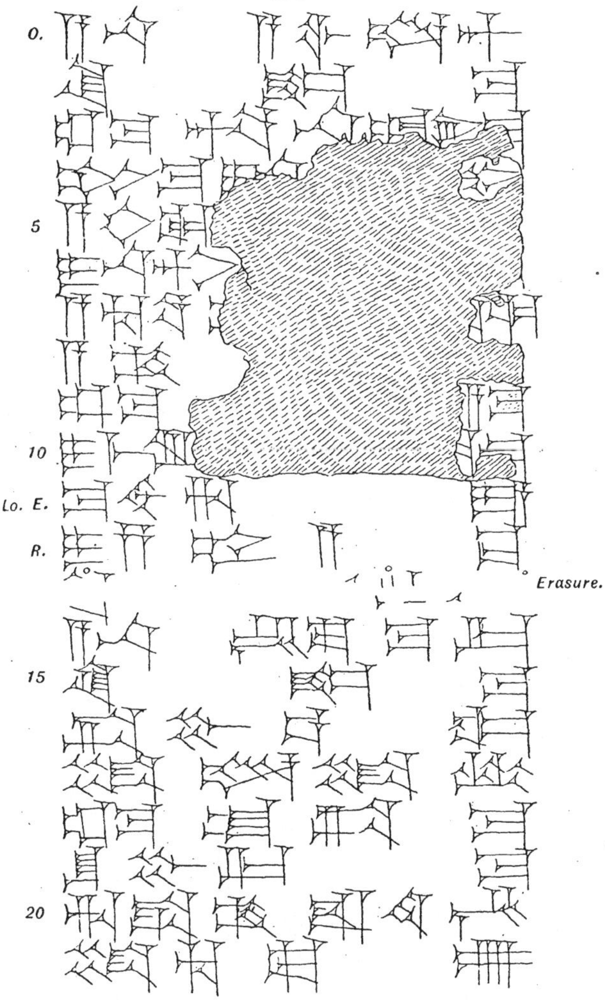

30

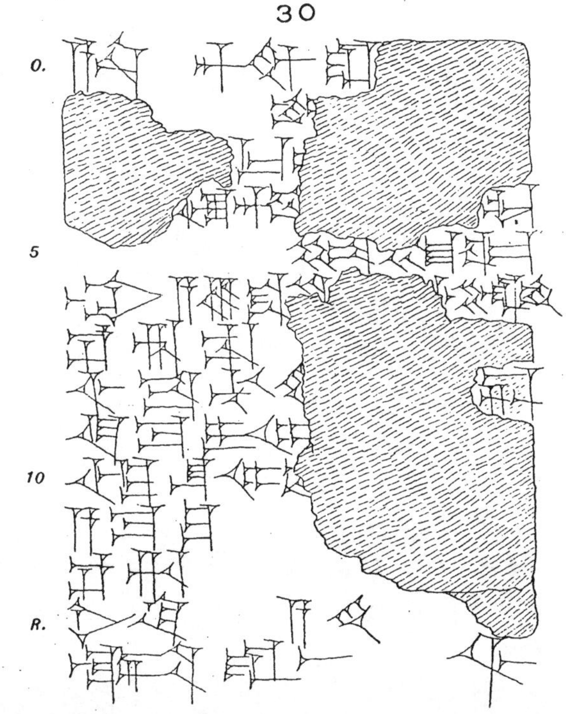

31

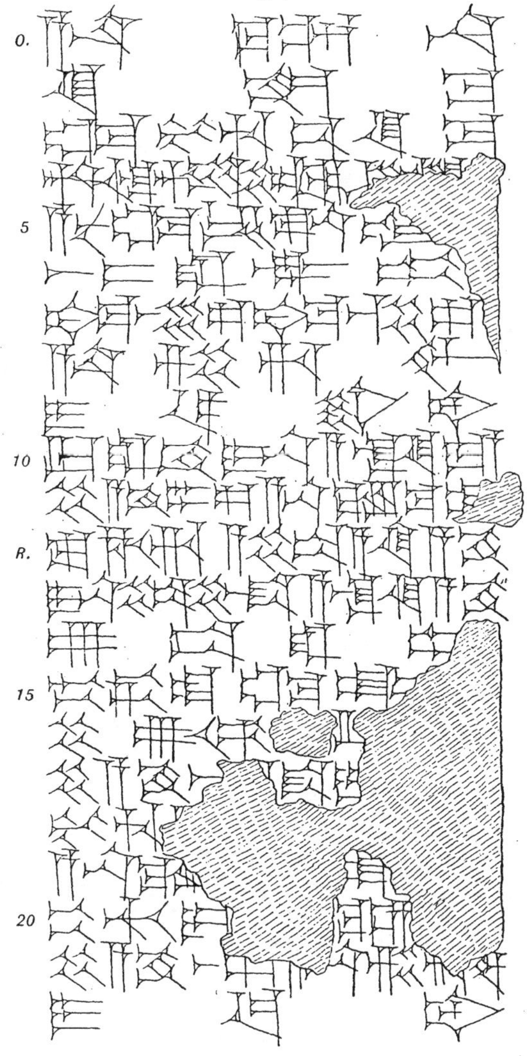

32

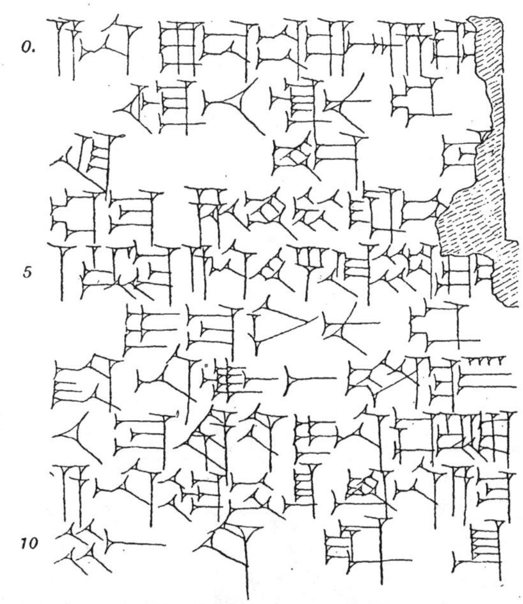

33

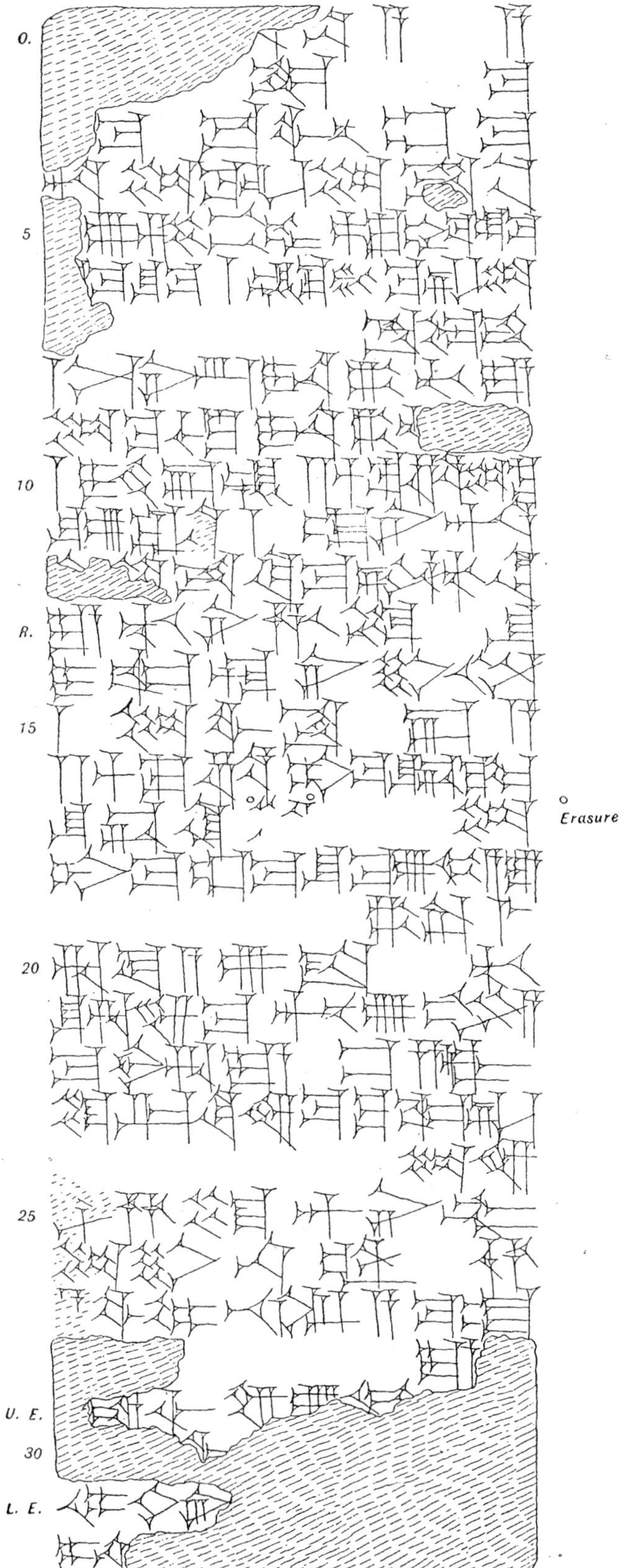

34

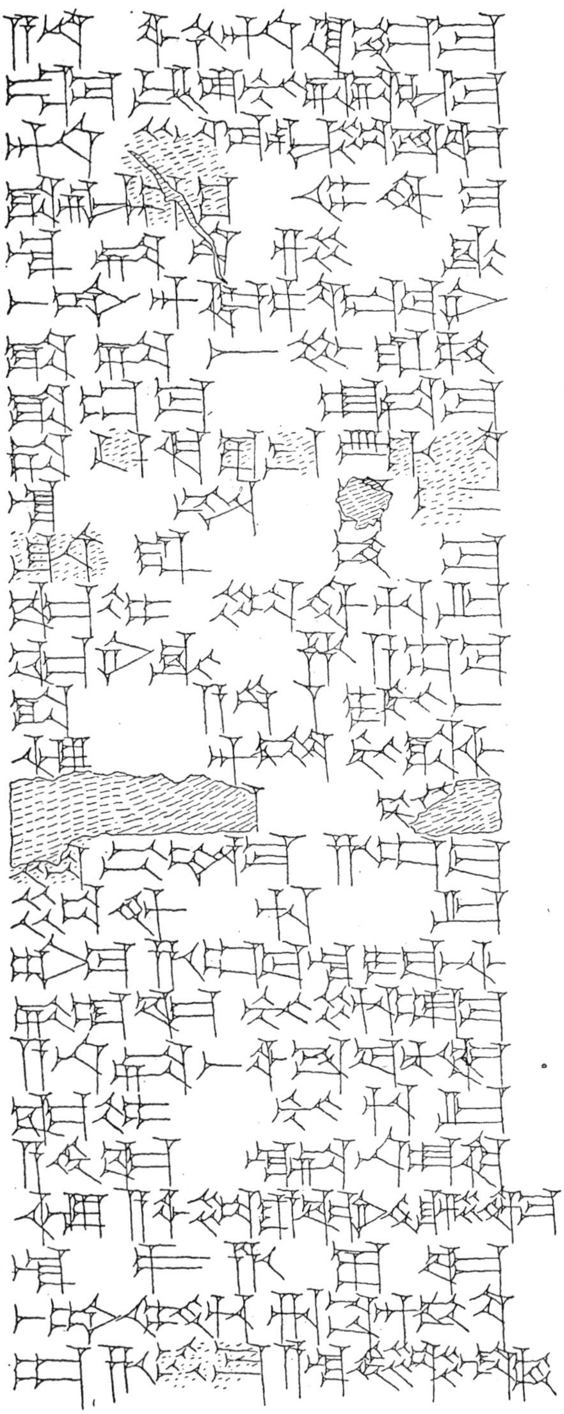

35

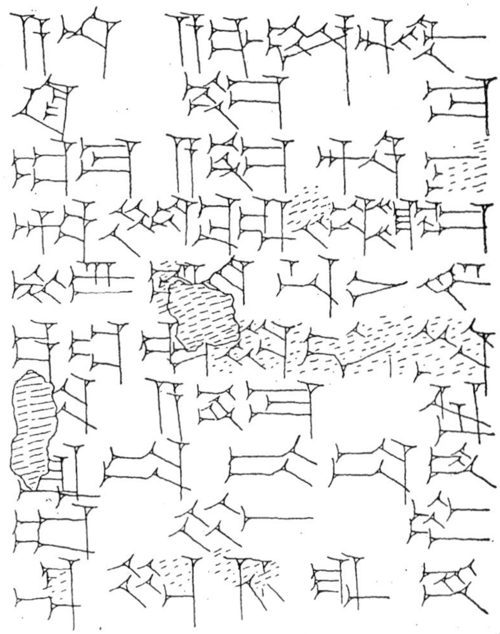

36

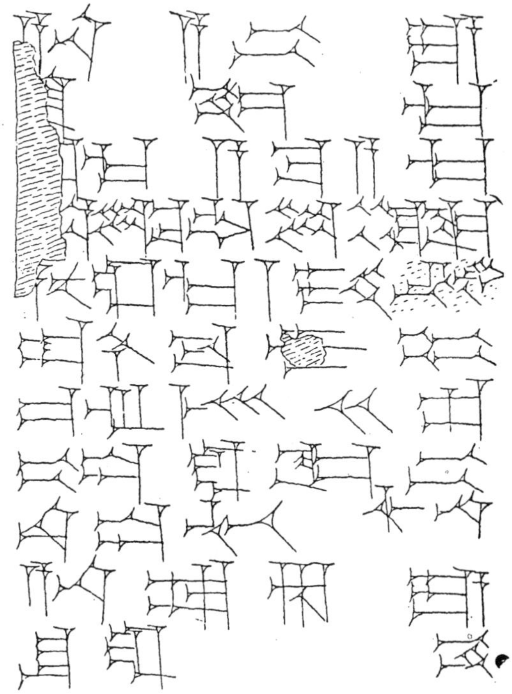

37

O.

R.

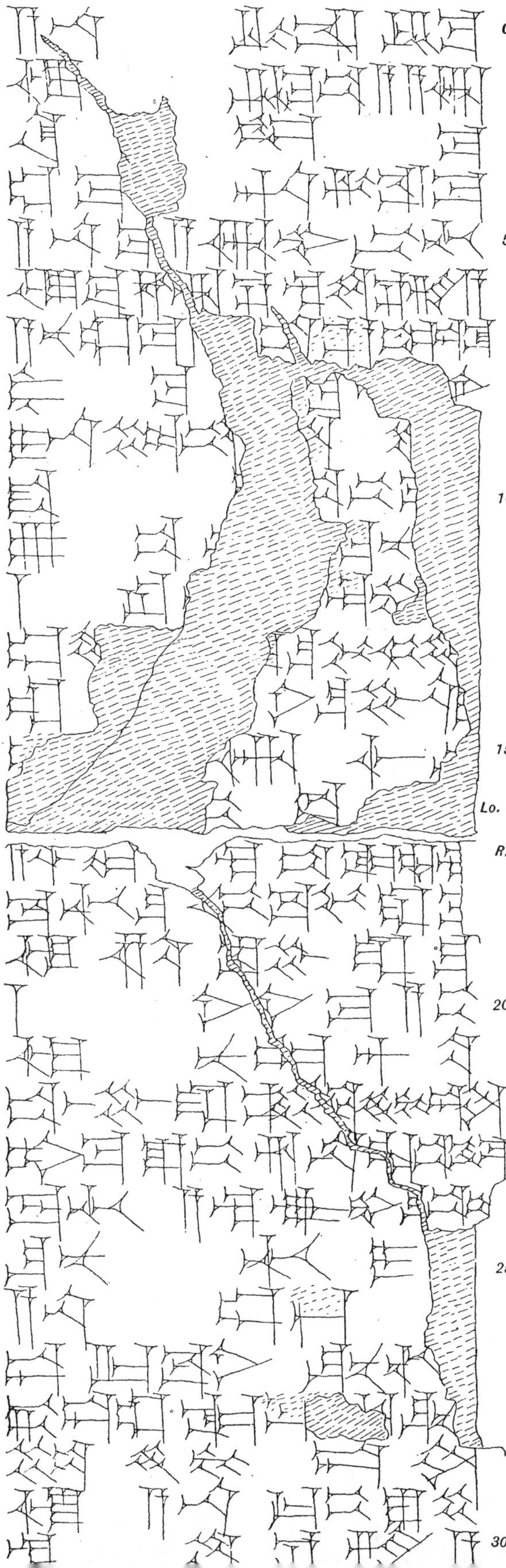

38

O.

Lo. E.

R.

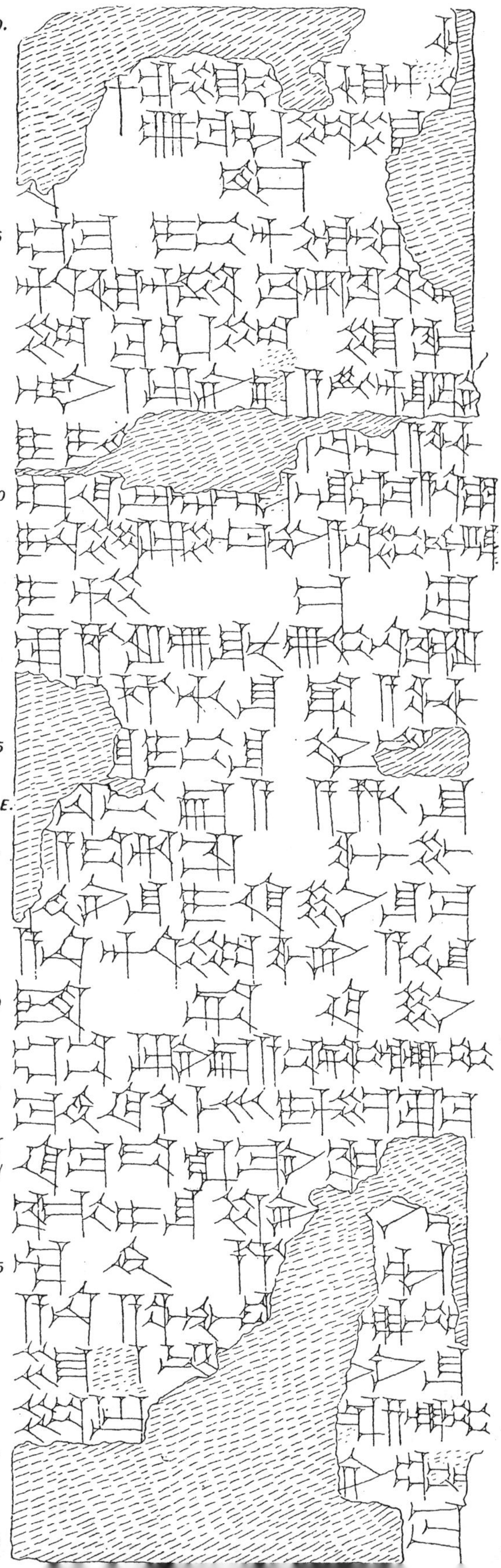

39

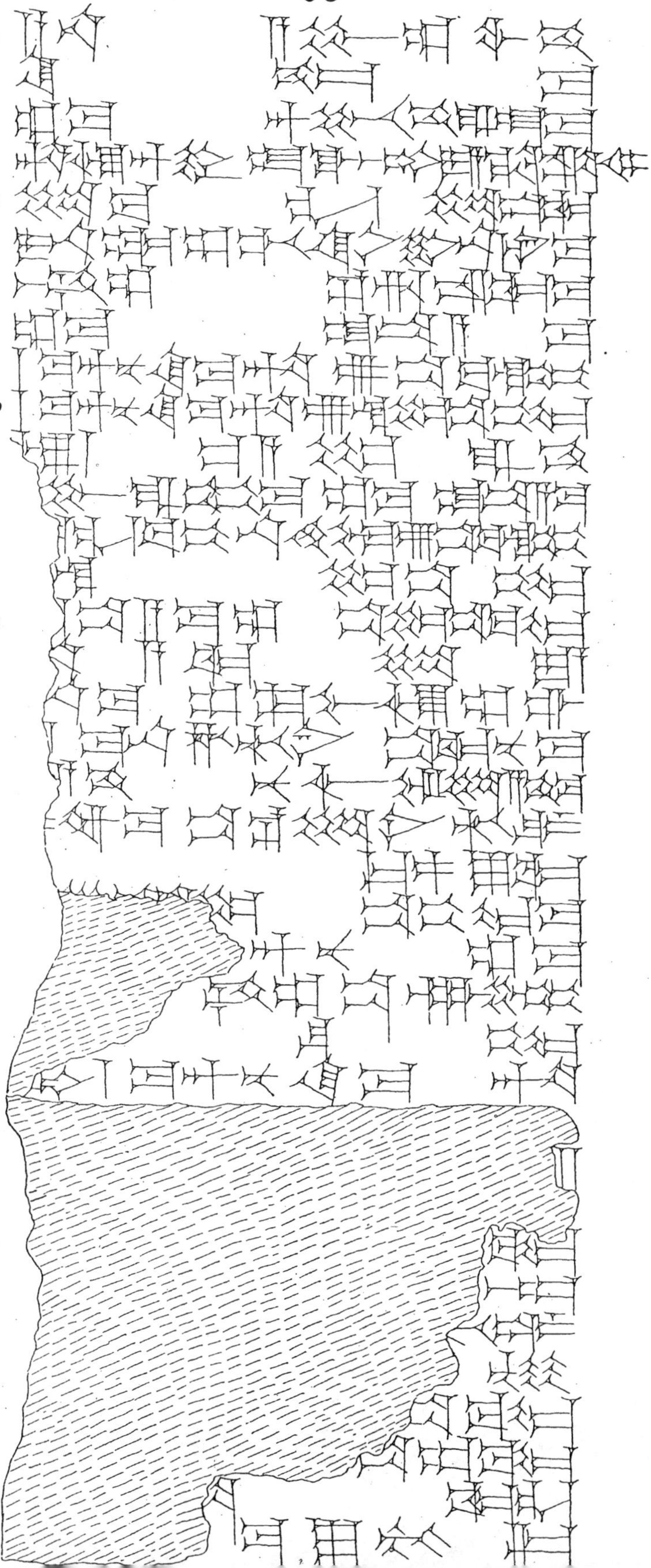

40

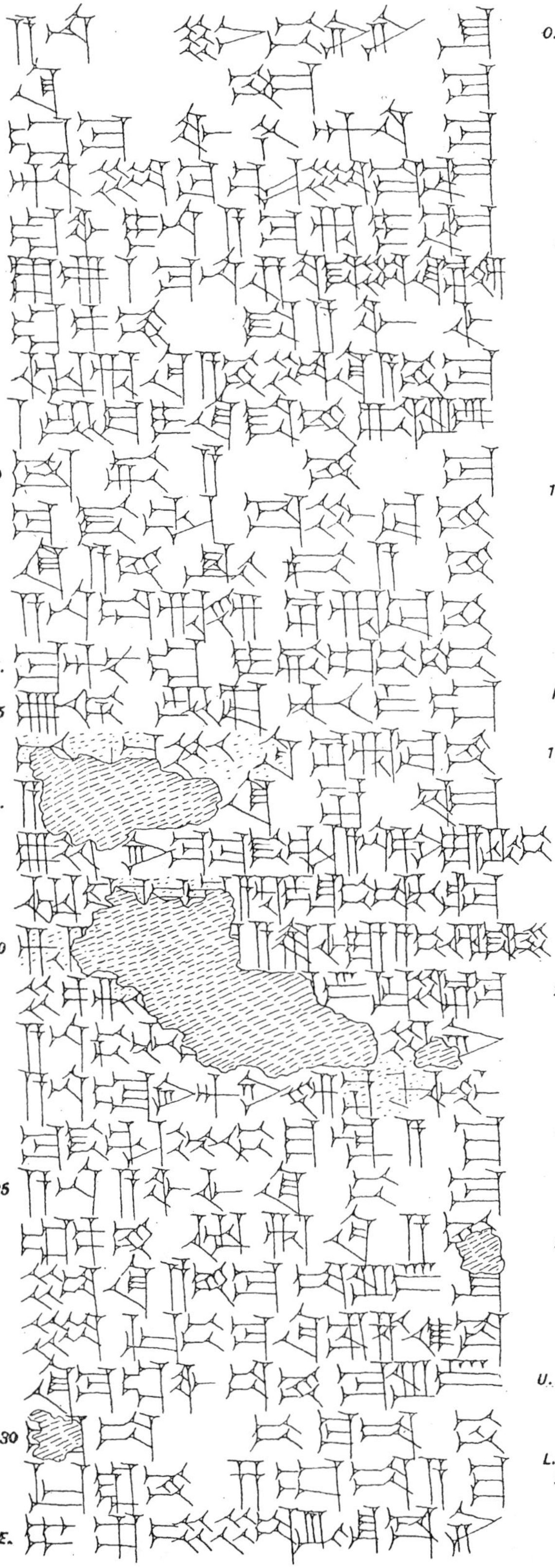

41

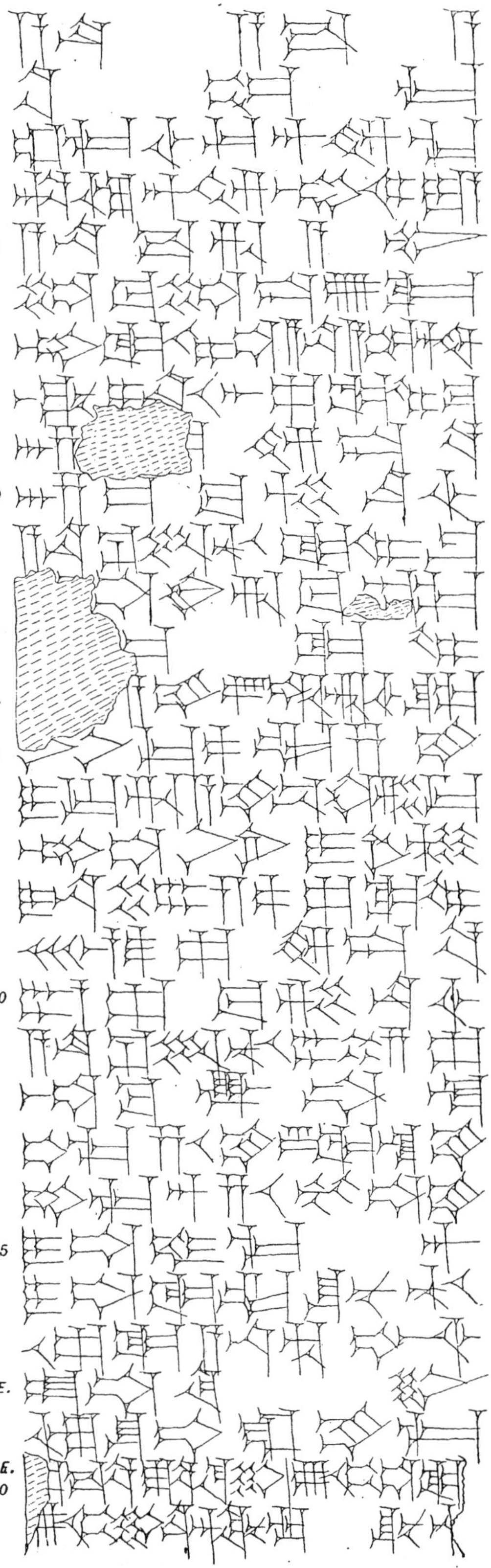

42

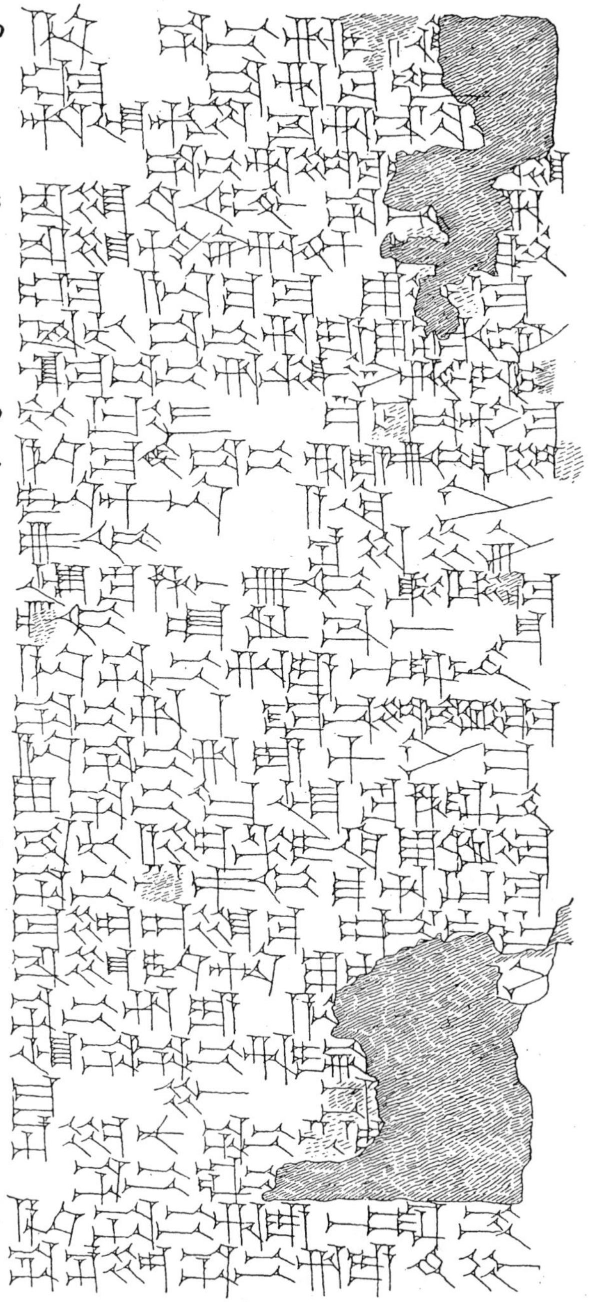

43

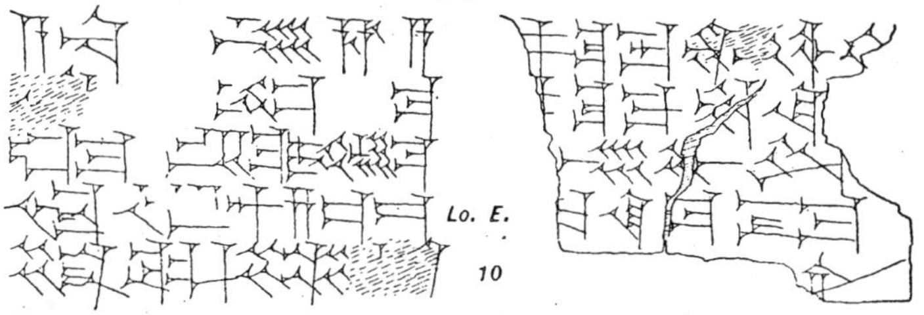

44

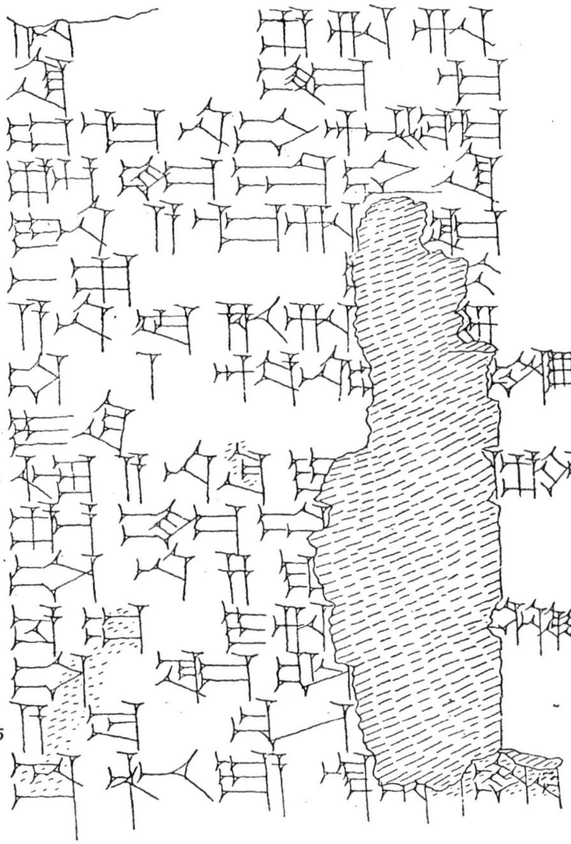

46

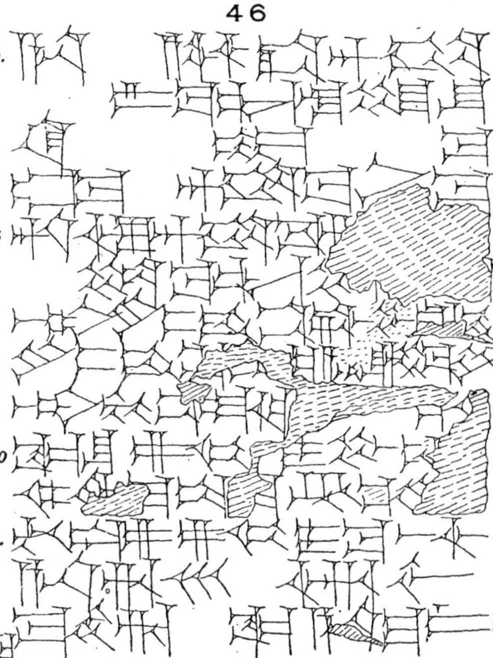

47

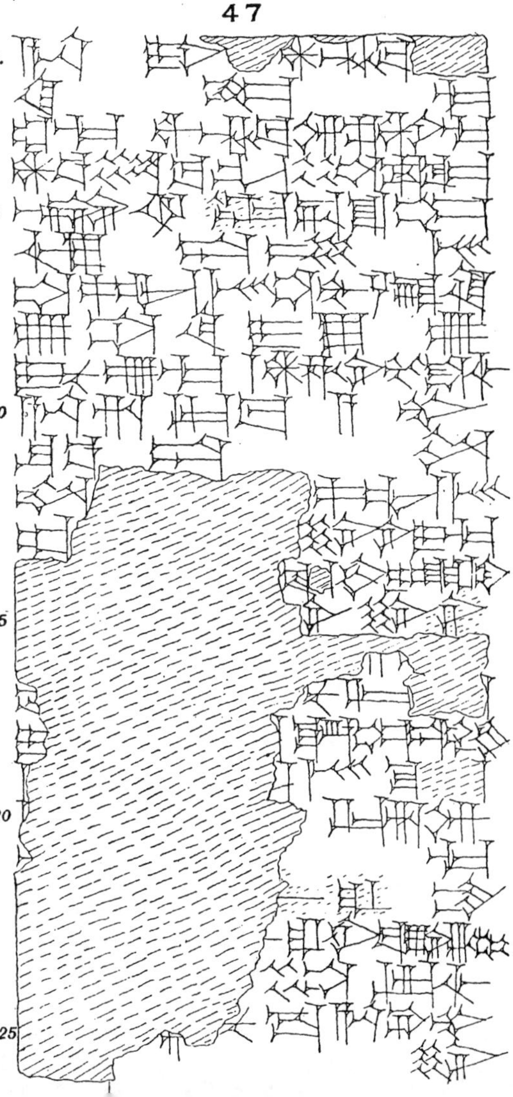

45

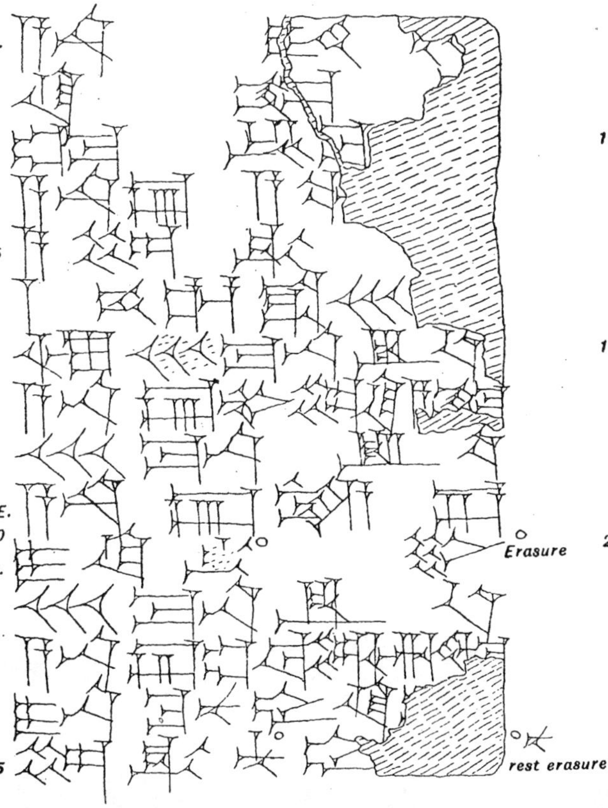

48

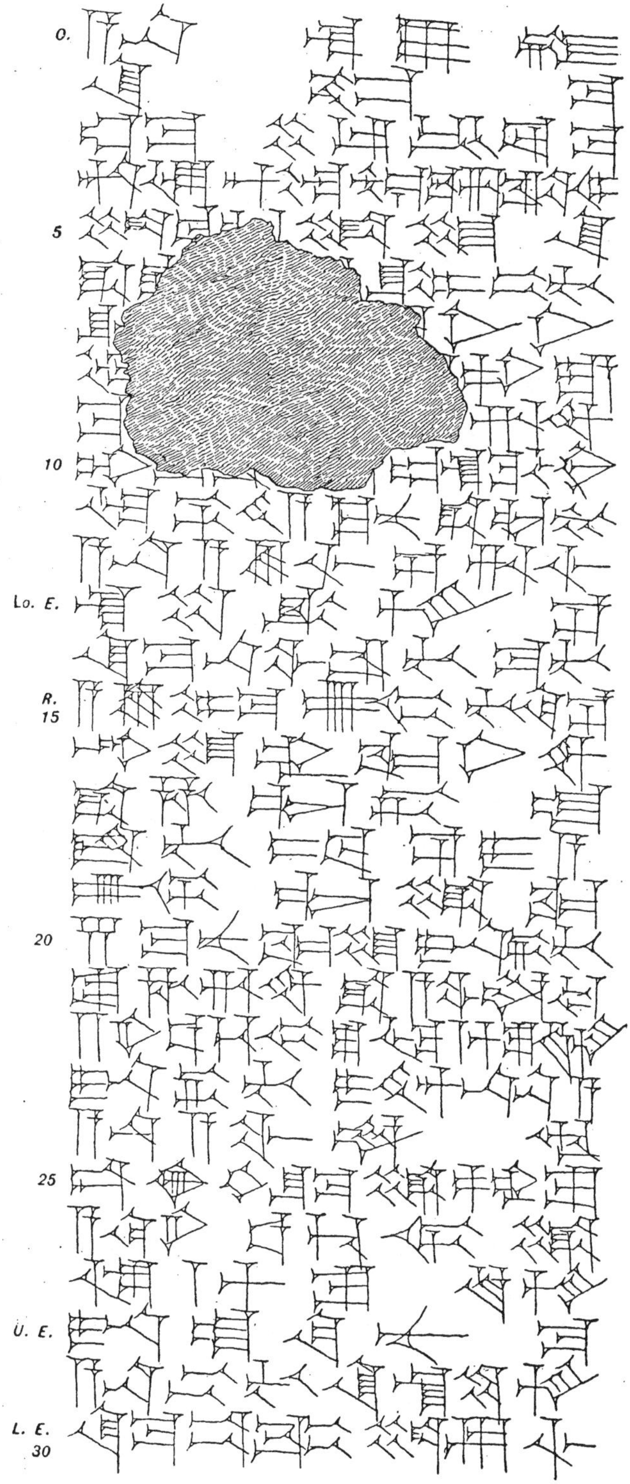

49

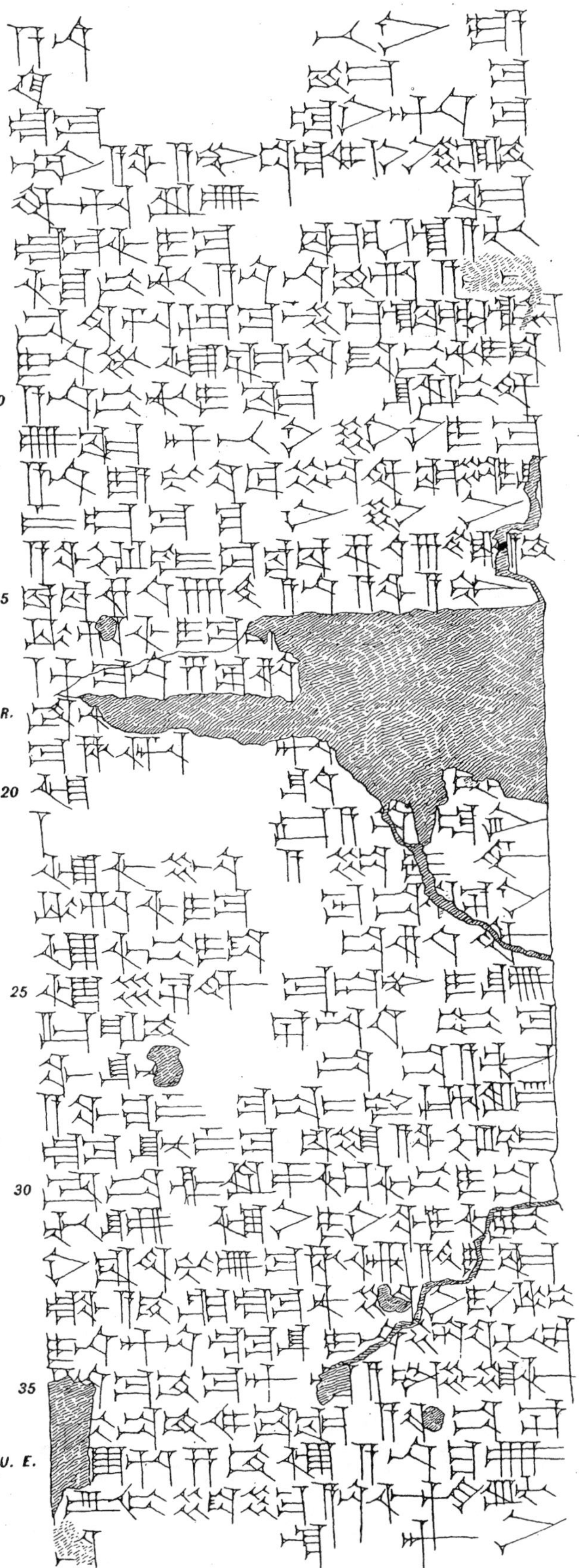

50

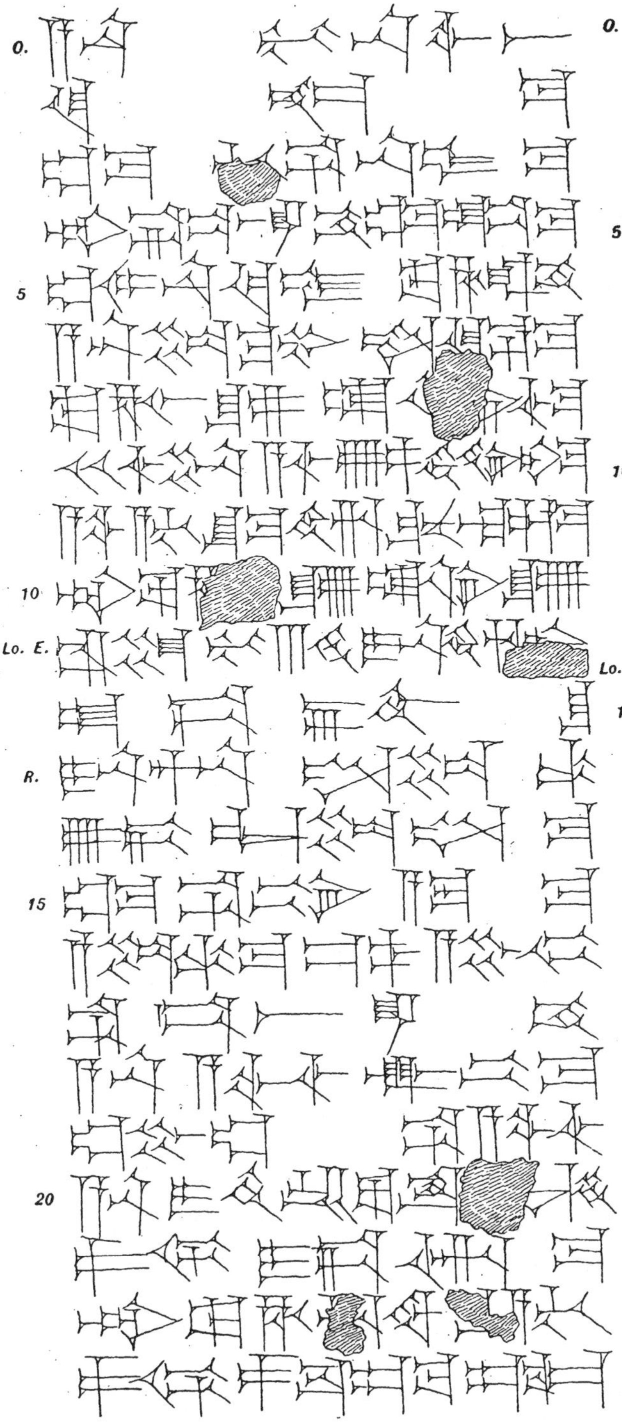

51

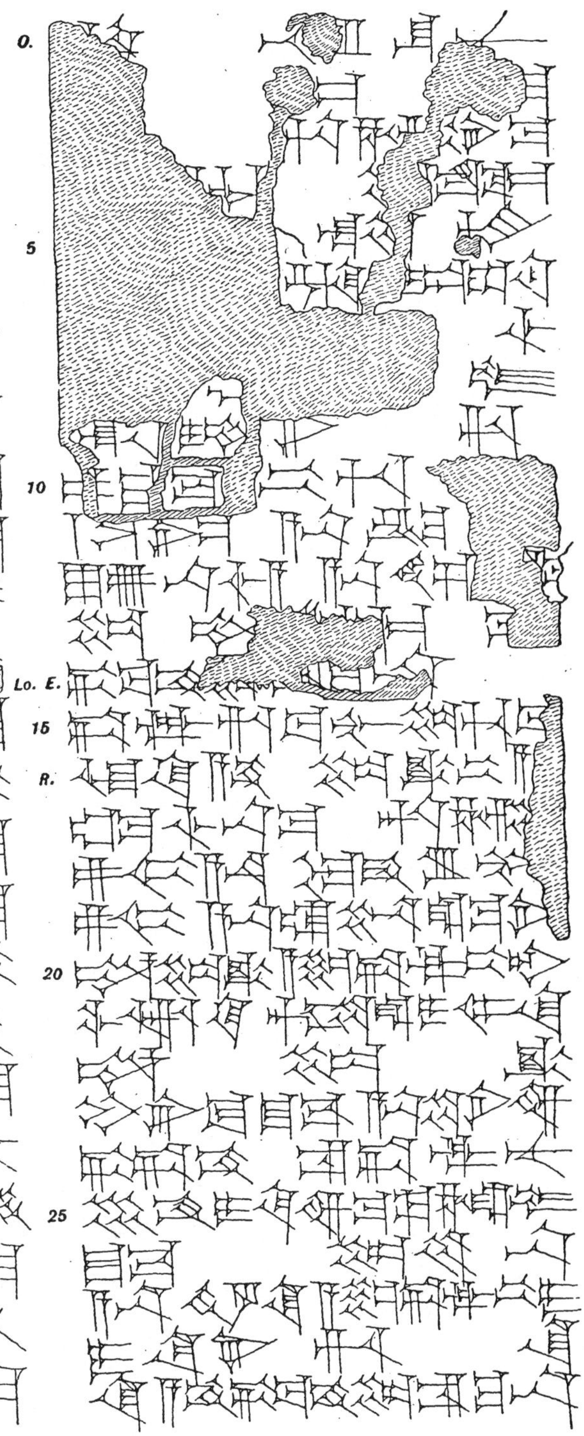

52

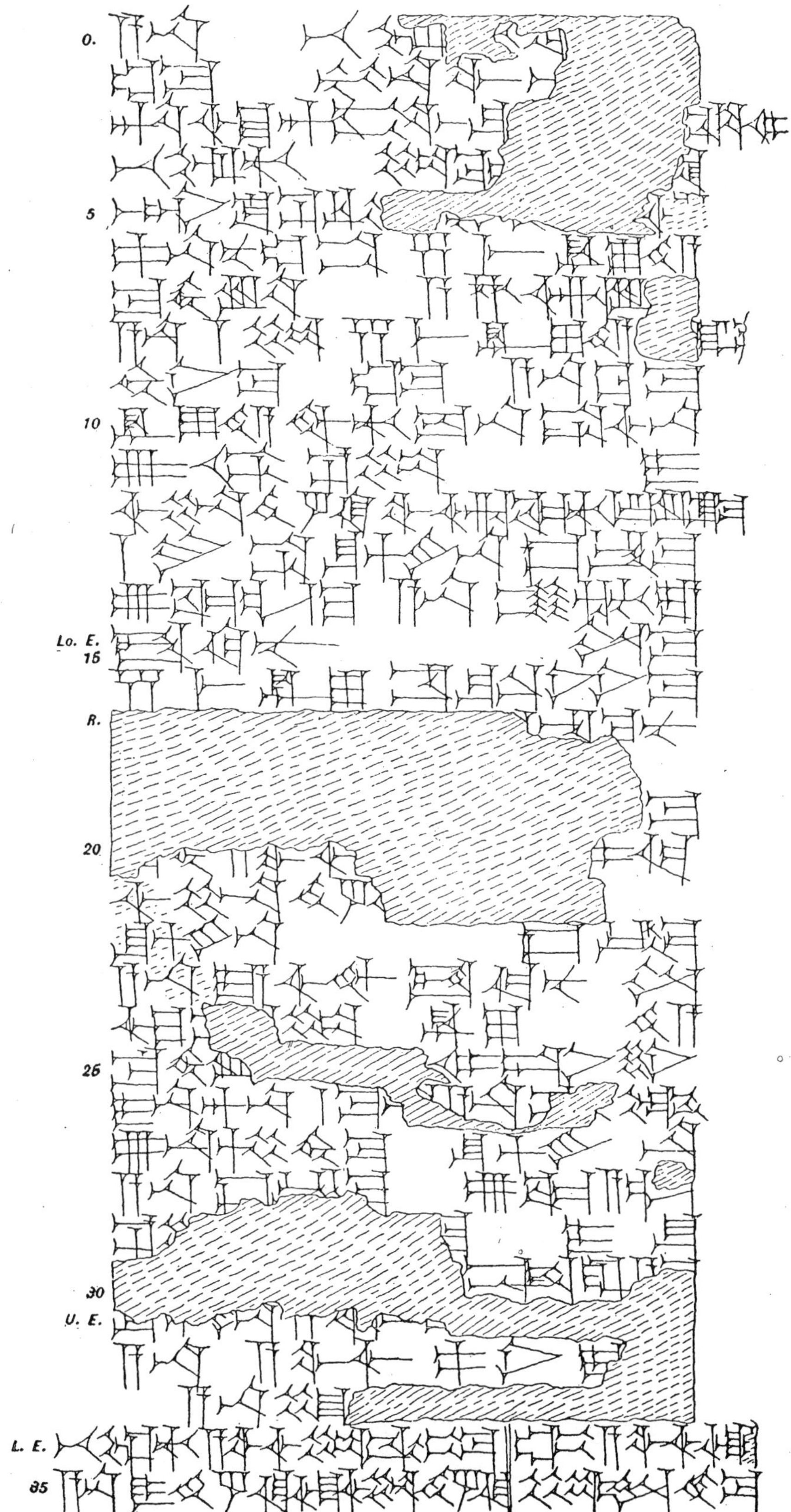

53

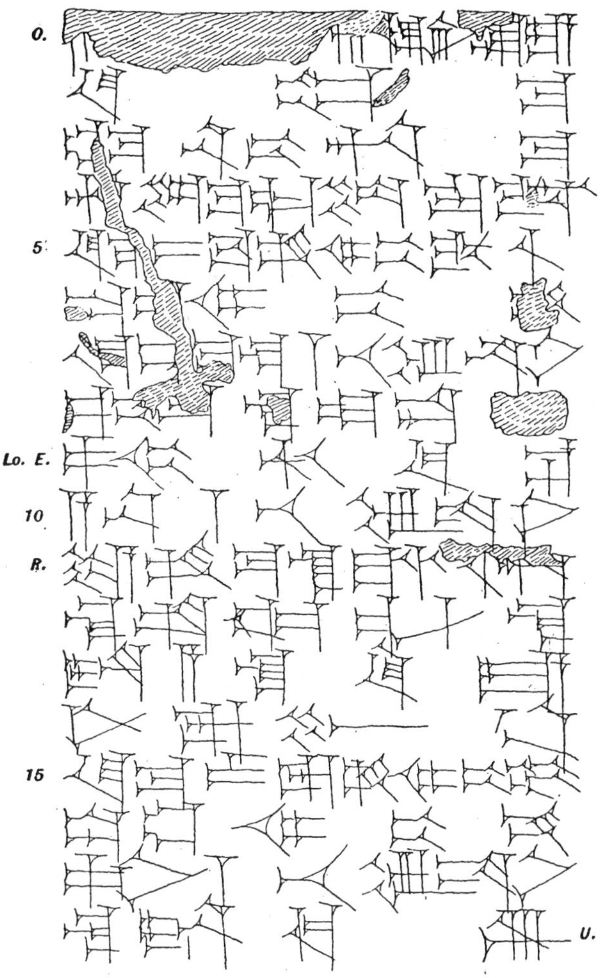

55

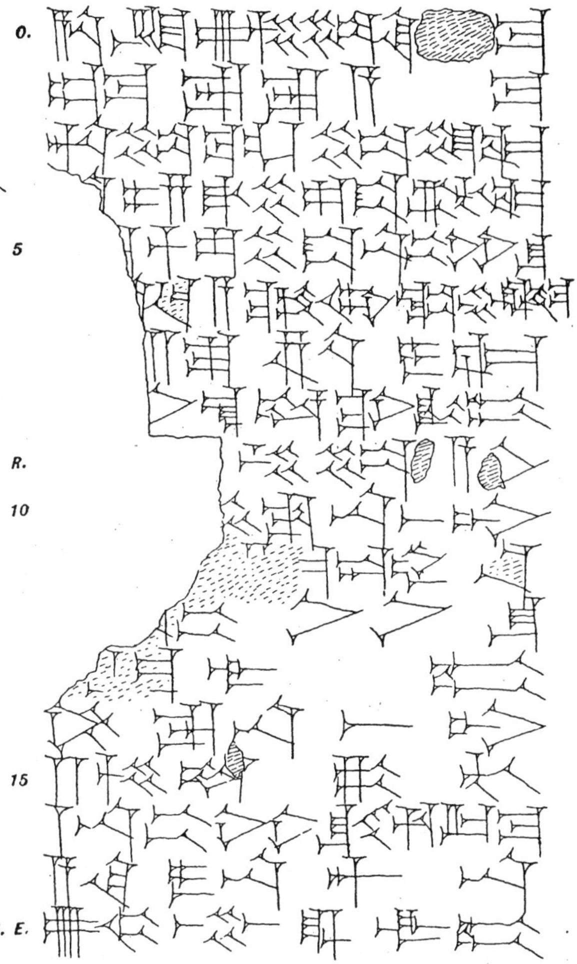

54

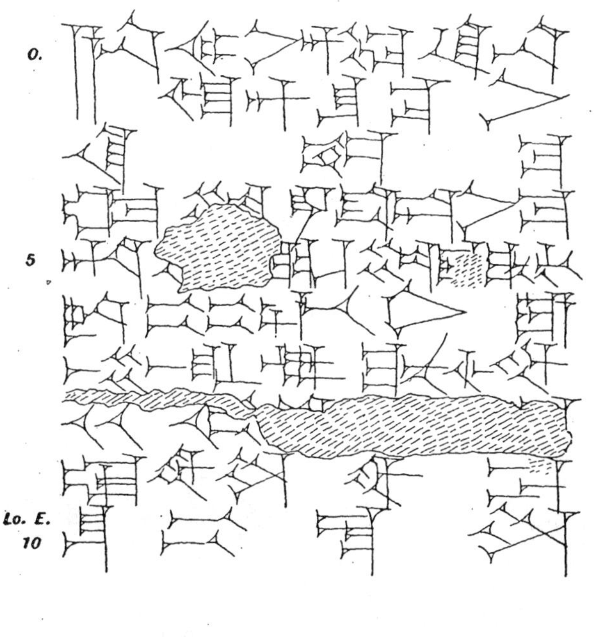

56

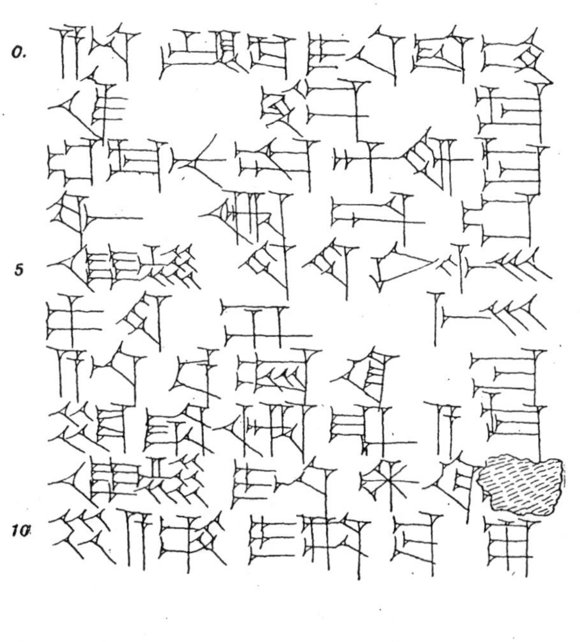

57

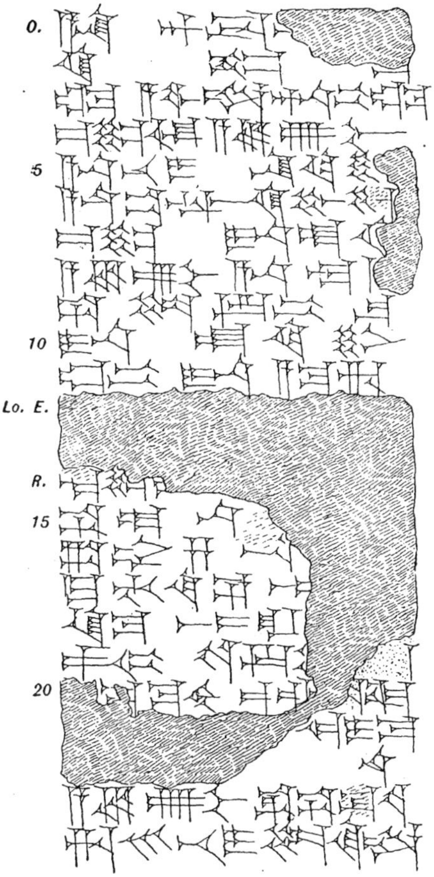

58

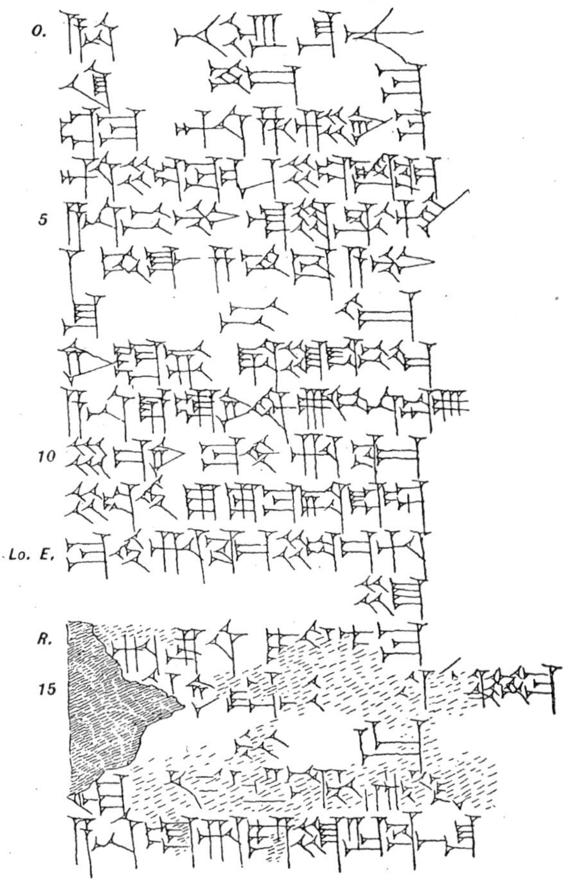

59

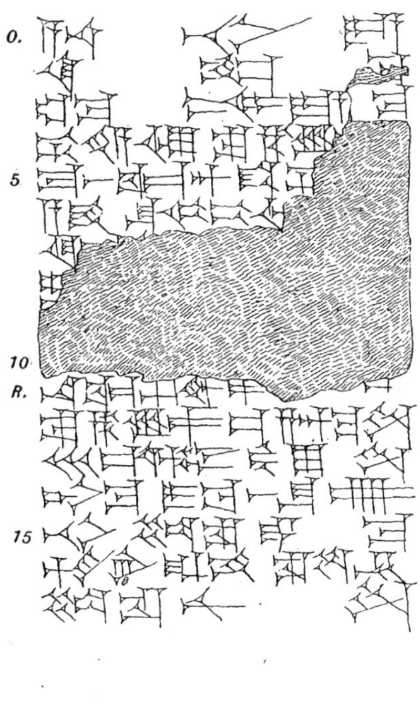

60

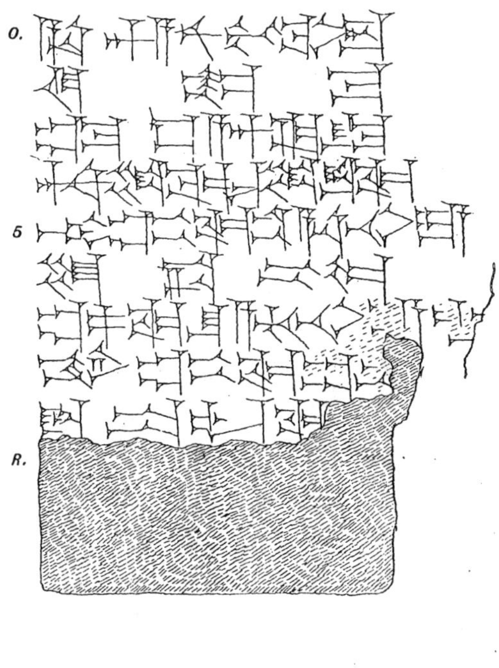

61

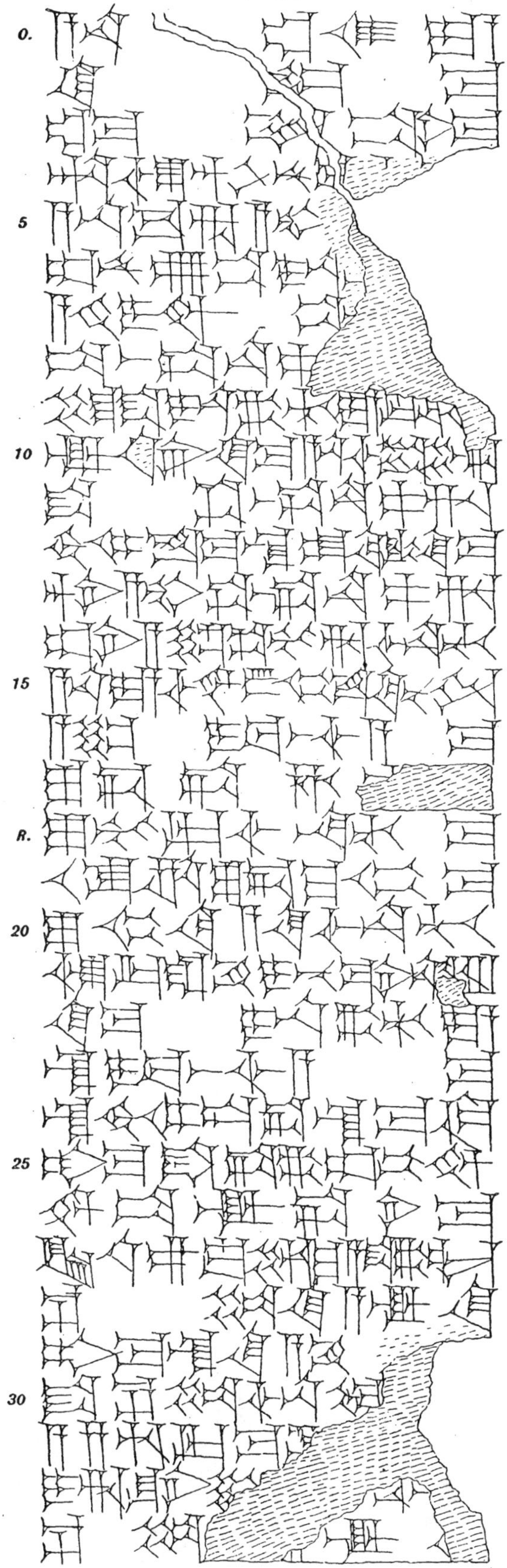

62

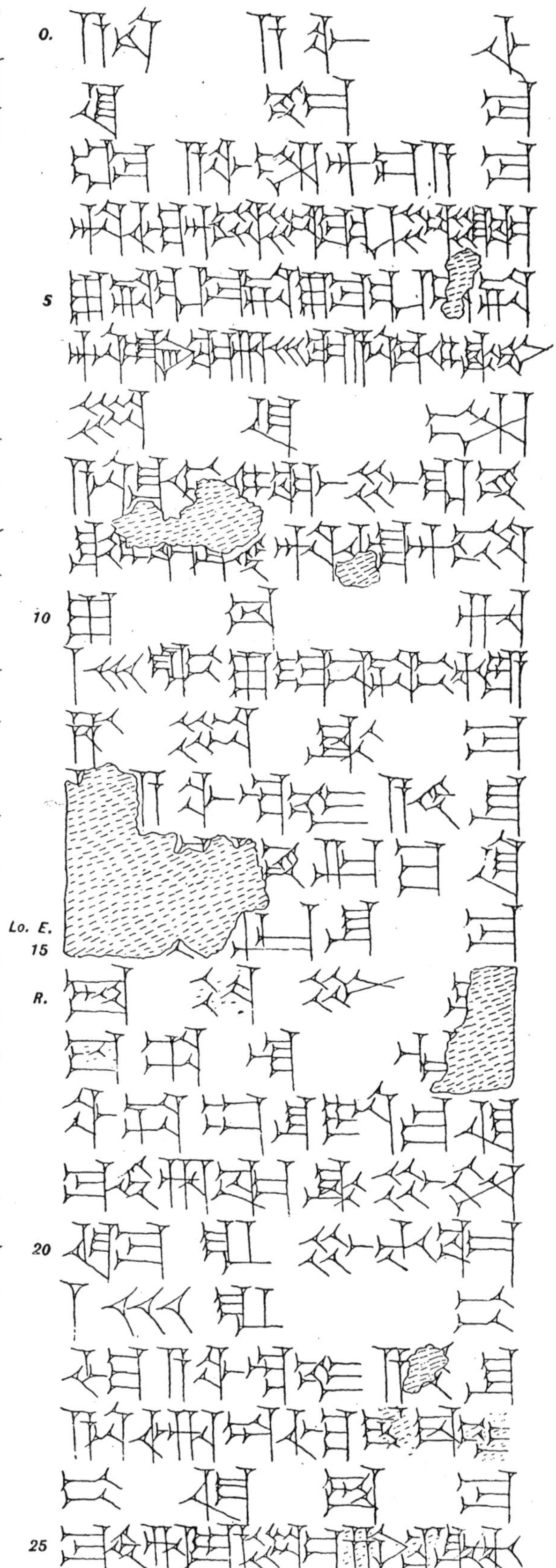

63

O.

Lo. E.

R.

U. E.

L. E.

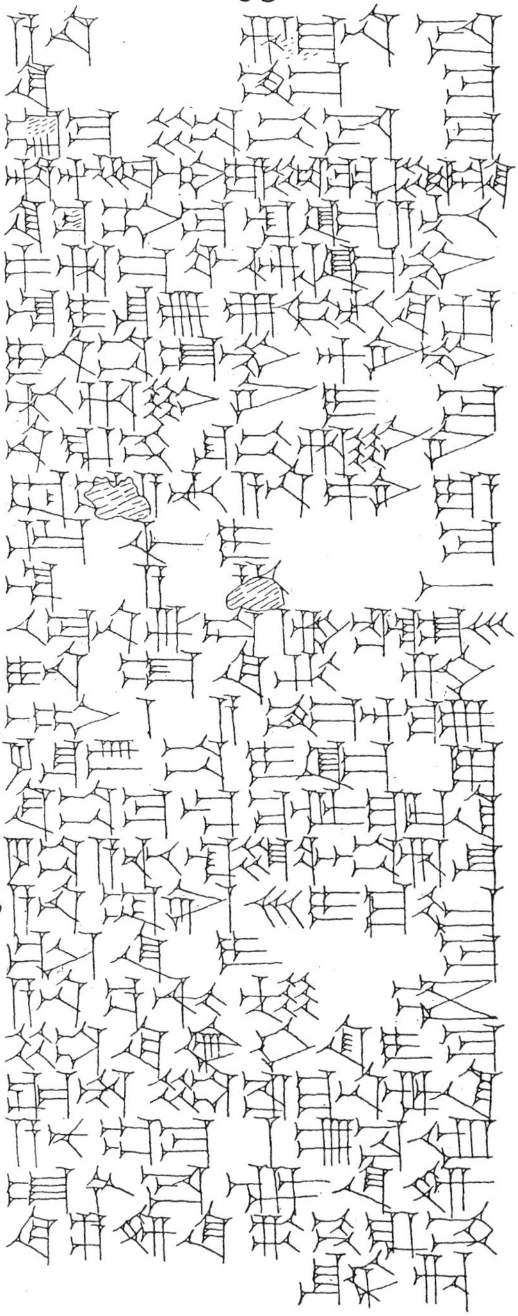

64

O.

R.

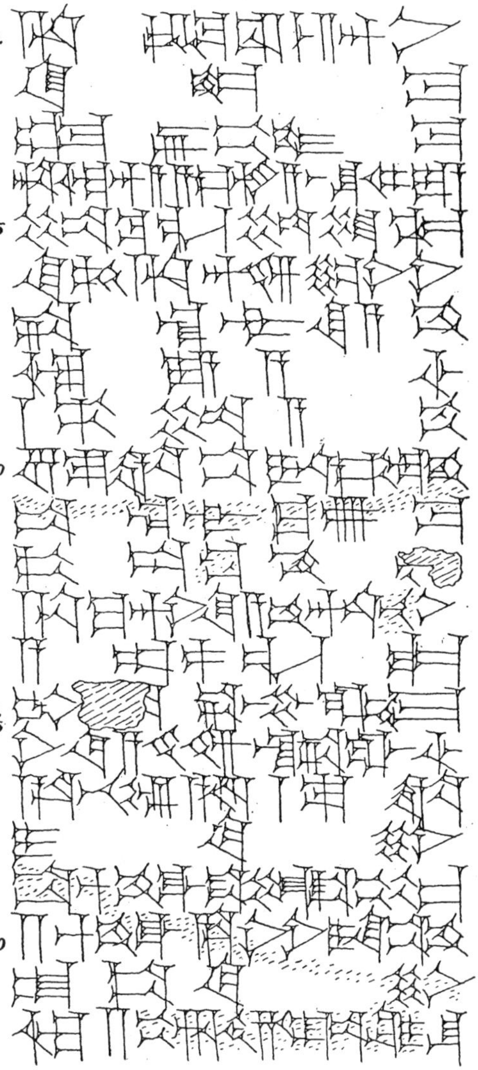

65

O.

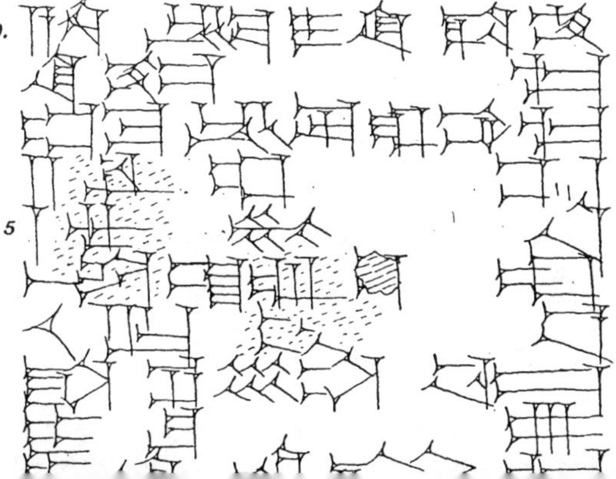

66

O.

Lo. E.

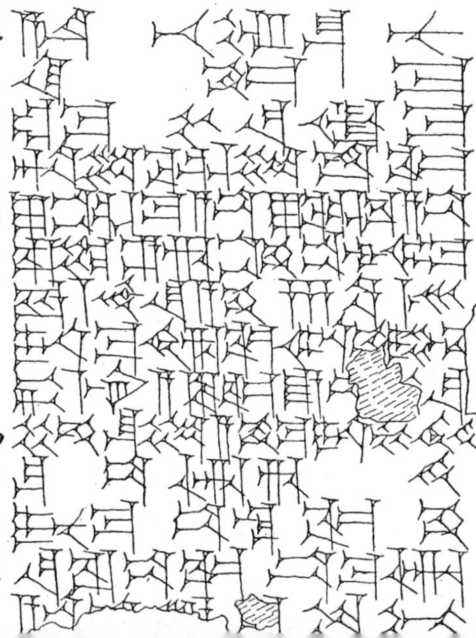

67

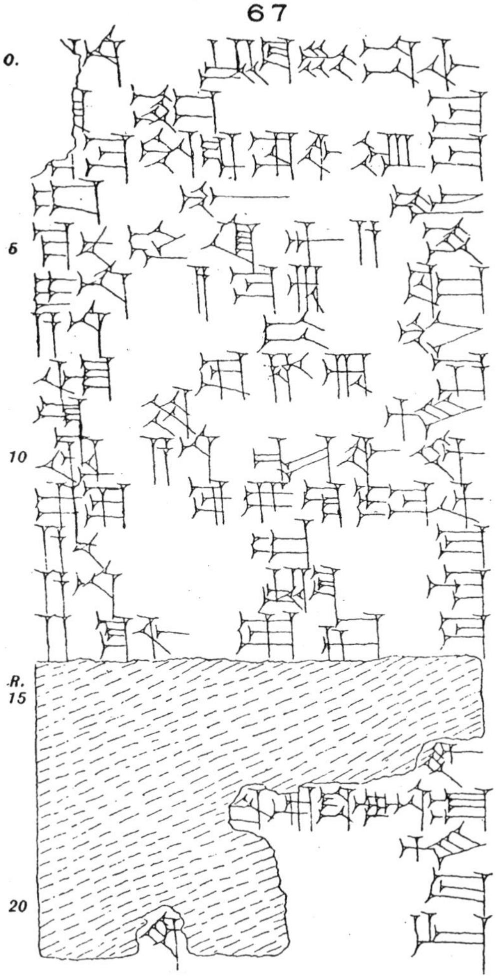

68

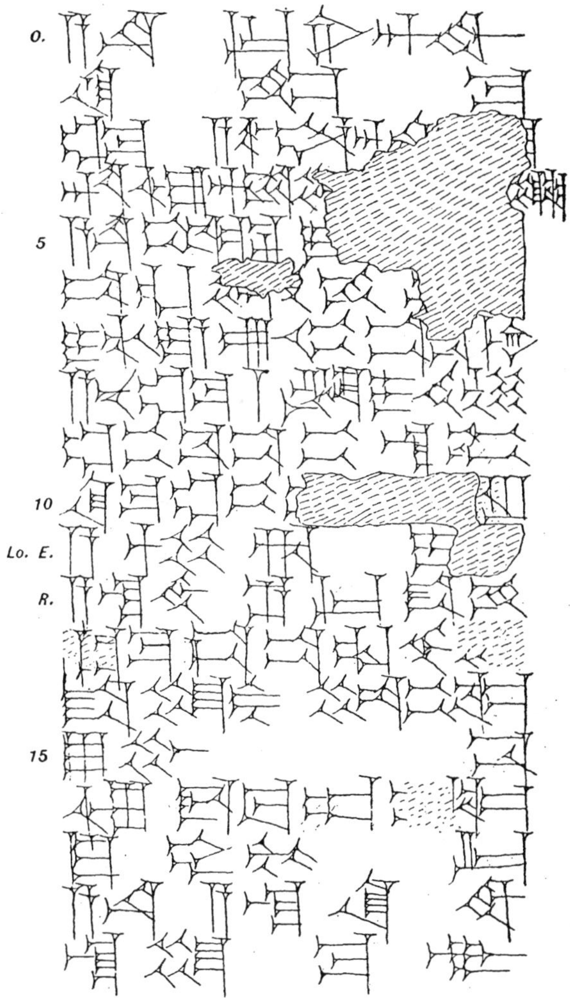

69

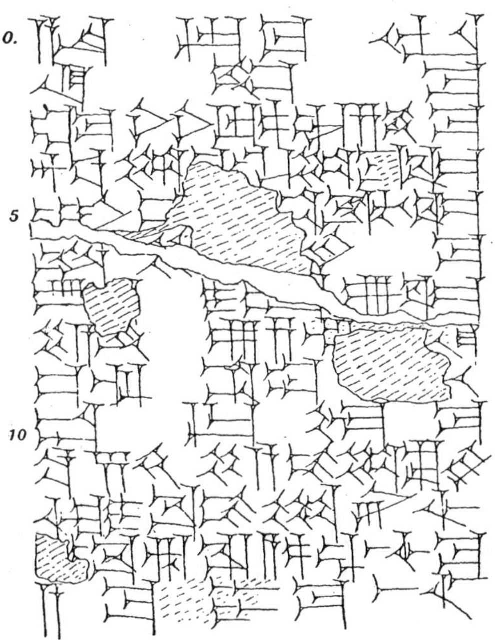

70

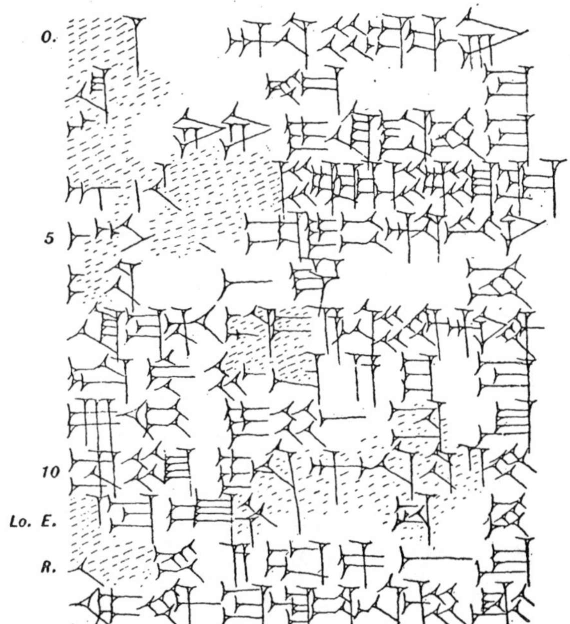

71

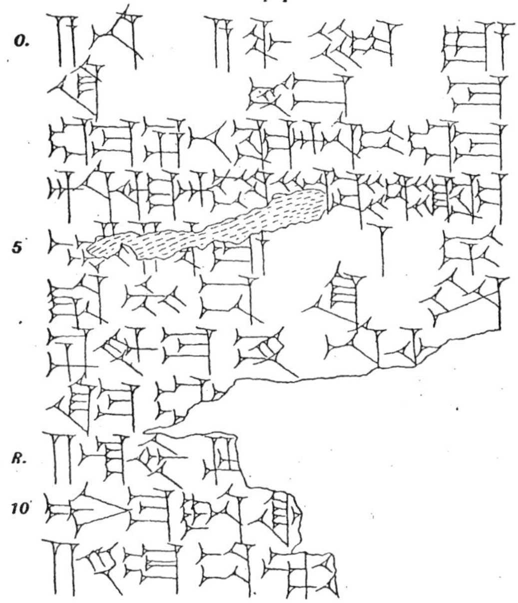

72

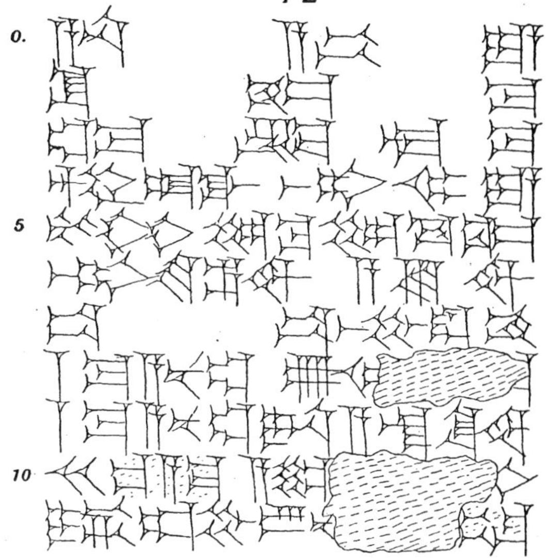

73

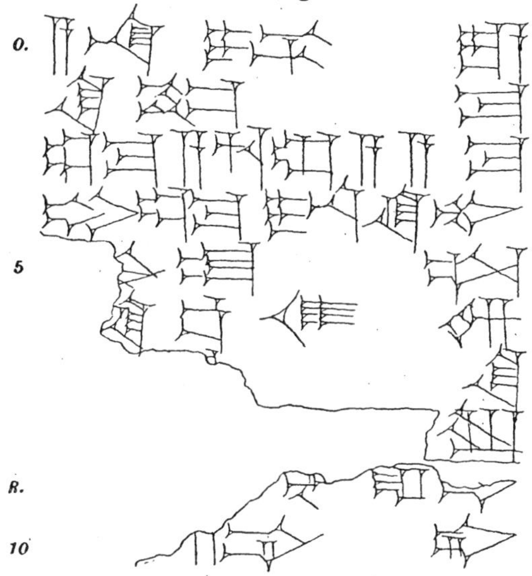

74

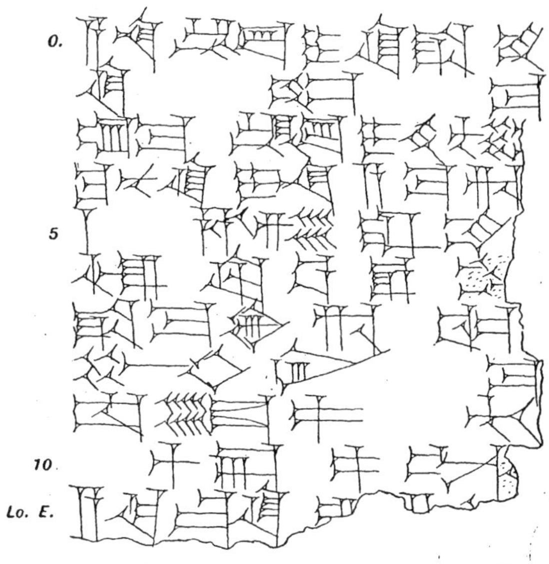

75

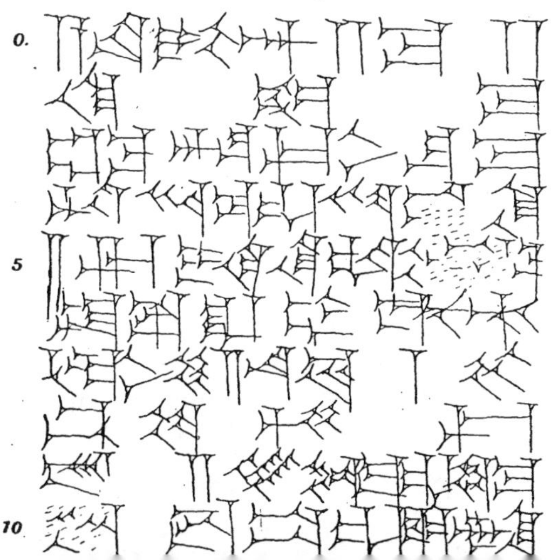

76

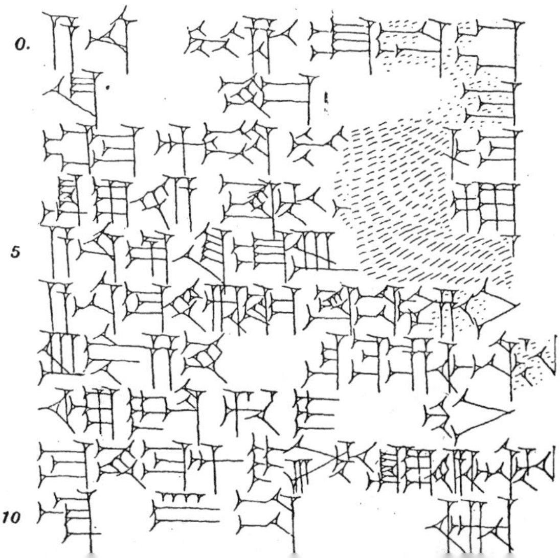

77

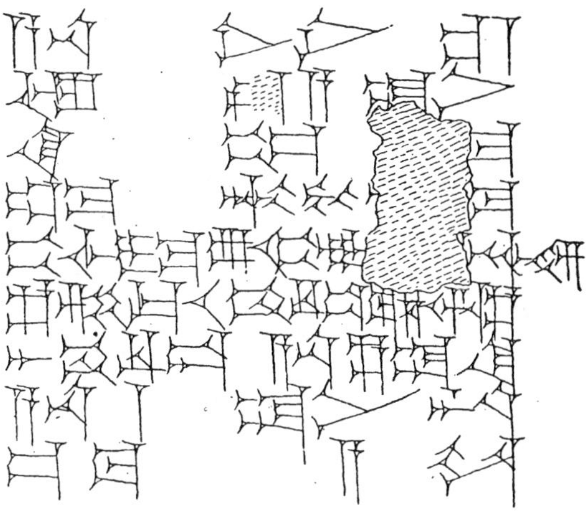
O.
5

78

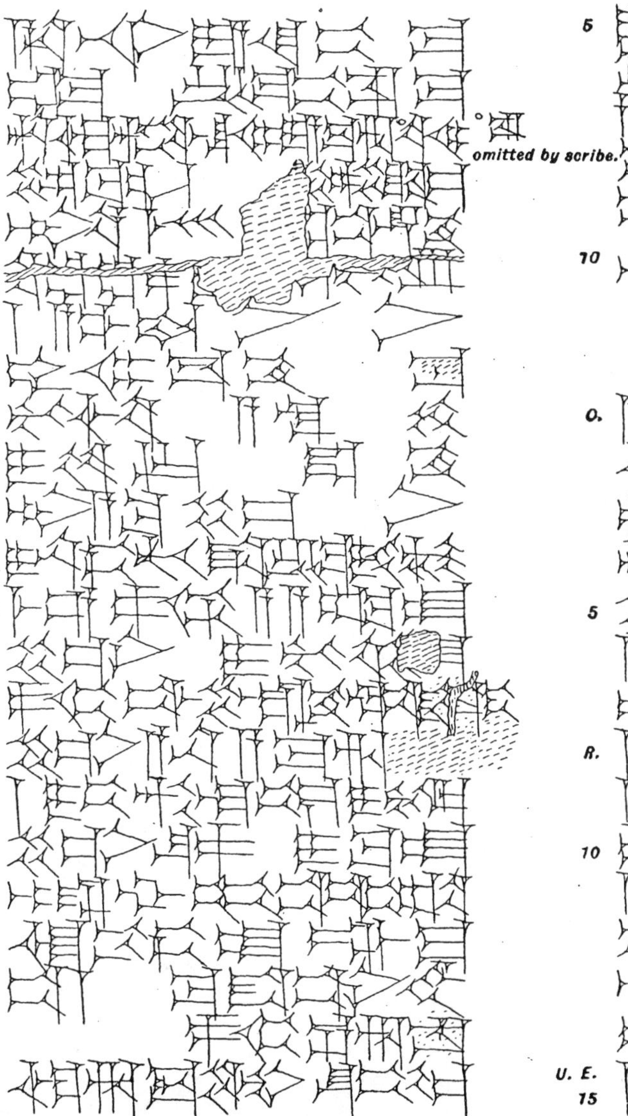
O.
5
Lo. E.
10
R.
15
U. E.
20
L. E.
omitted by scribe.

79

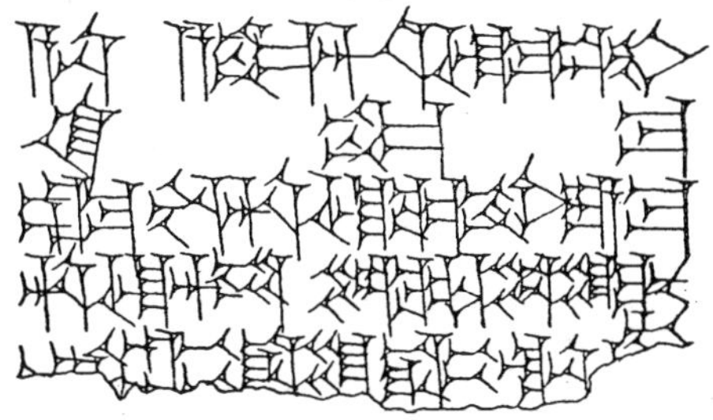
O.
5

80

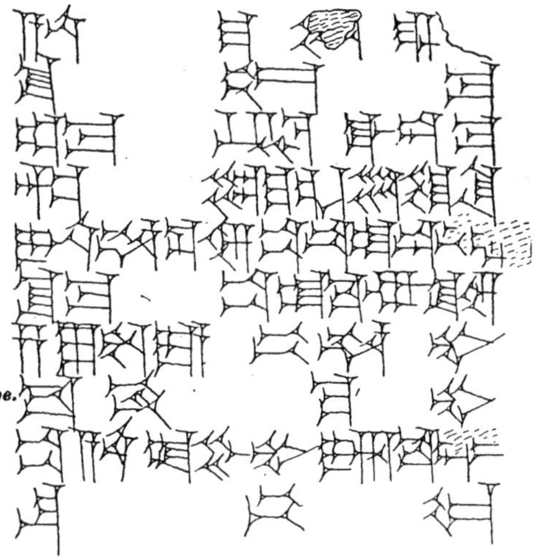
O.
5
10

81

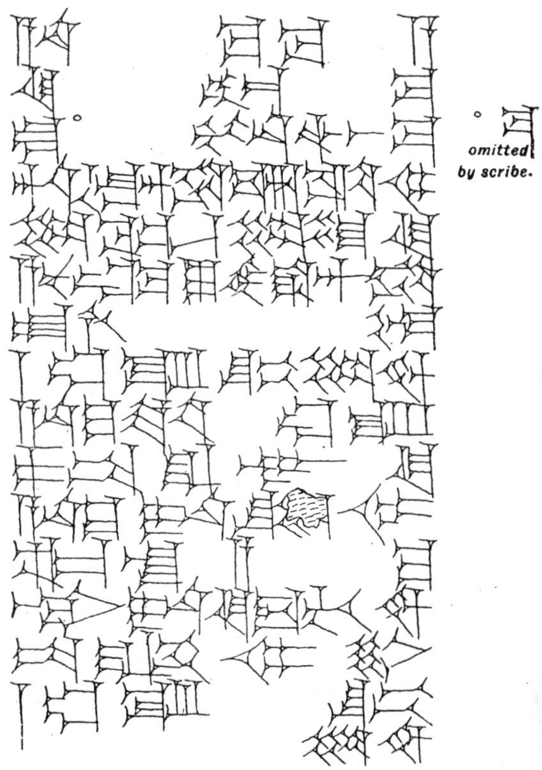
O.
5
R.
10
U. E.
15
omitted by scribe.

82

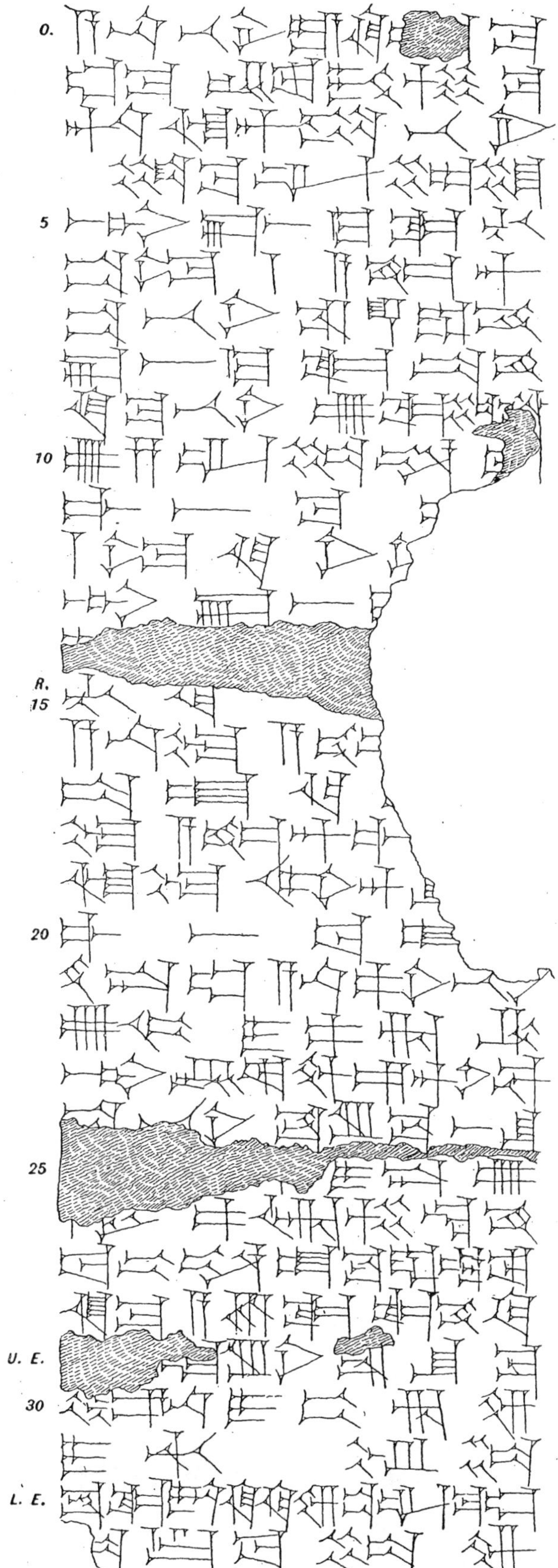

83

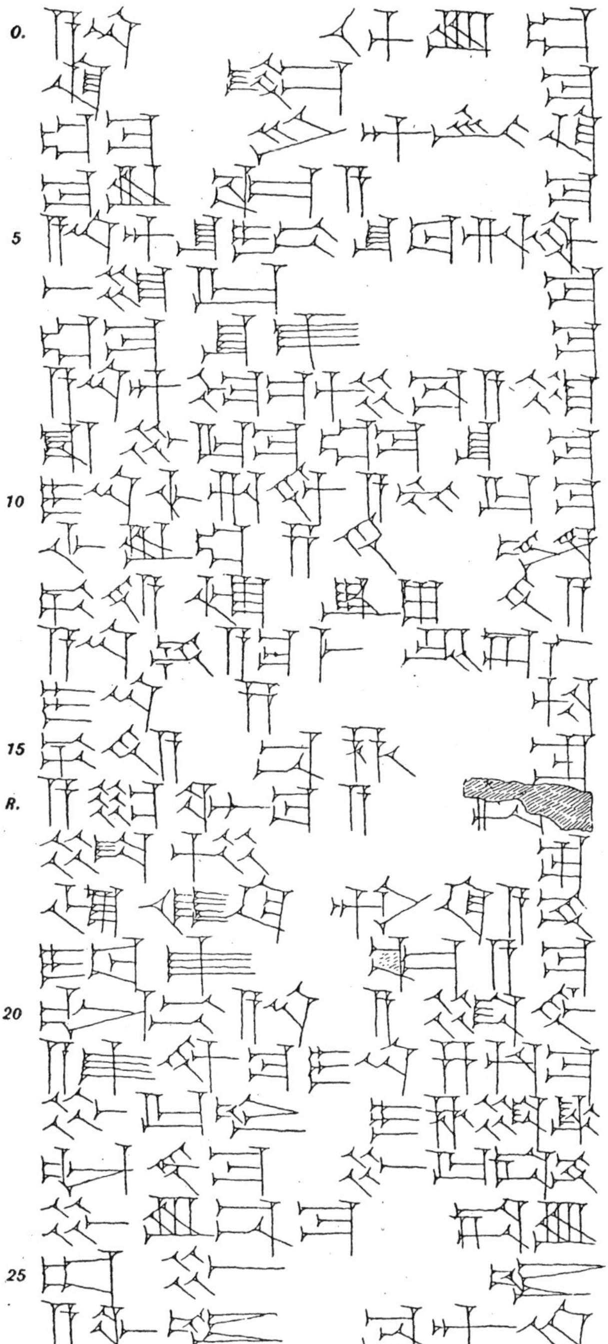

84

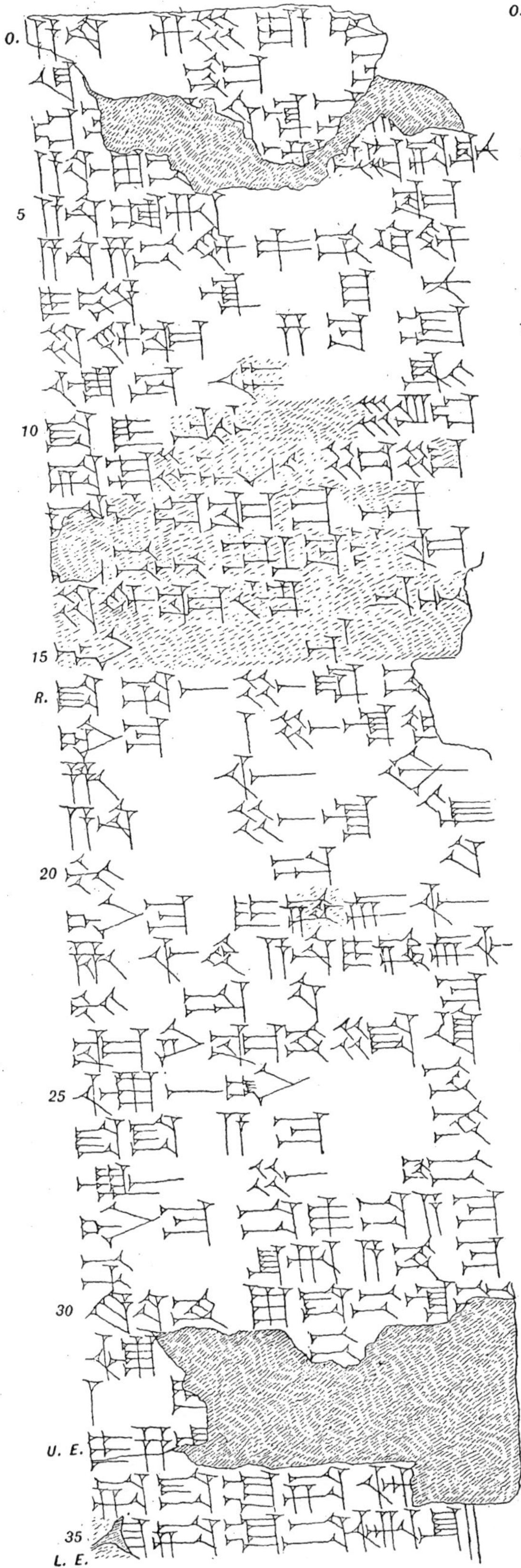

85

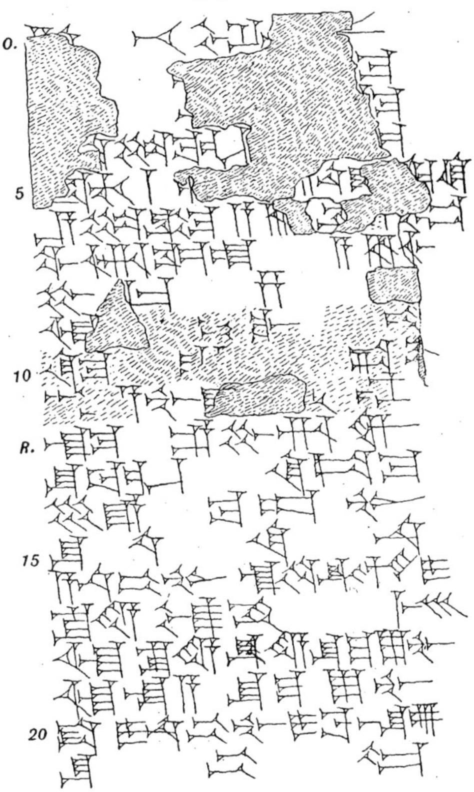

86

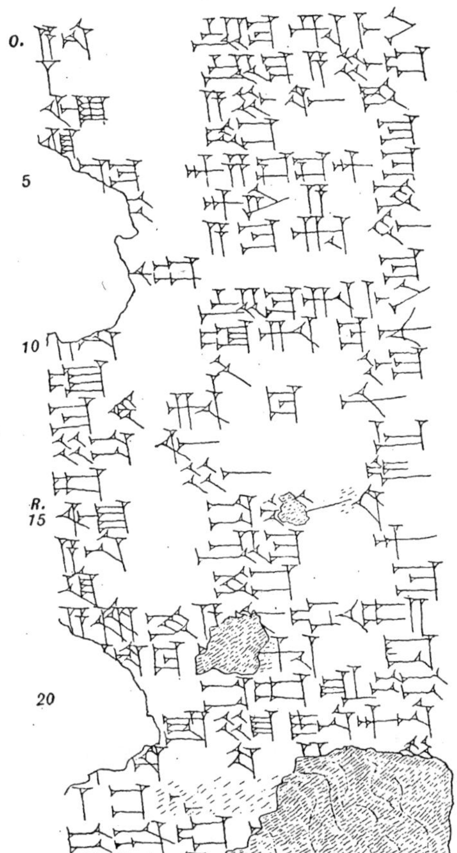

92

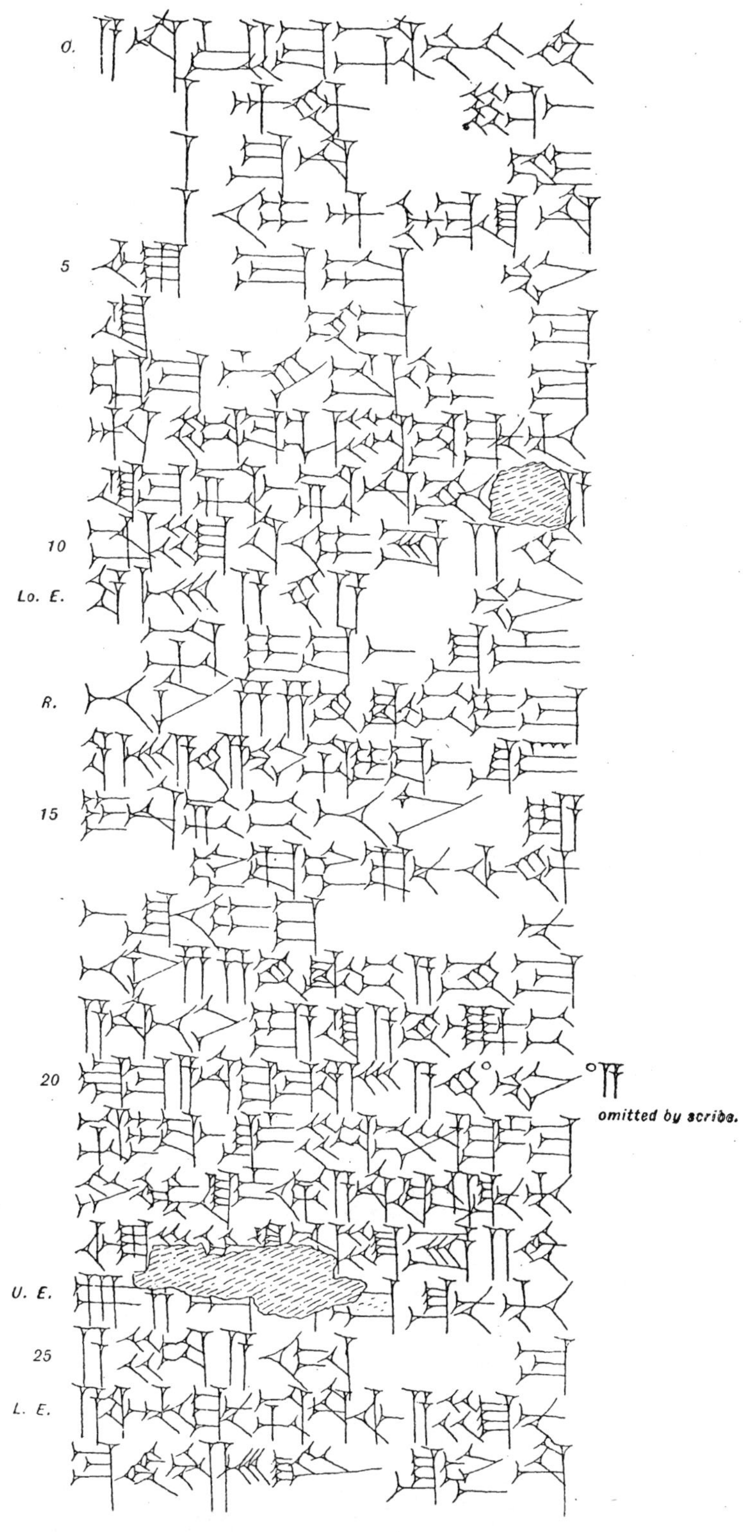

93

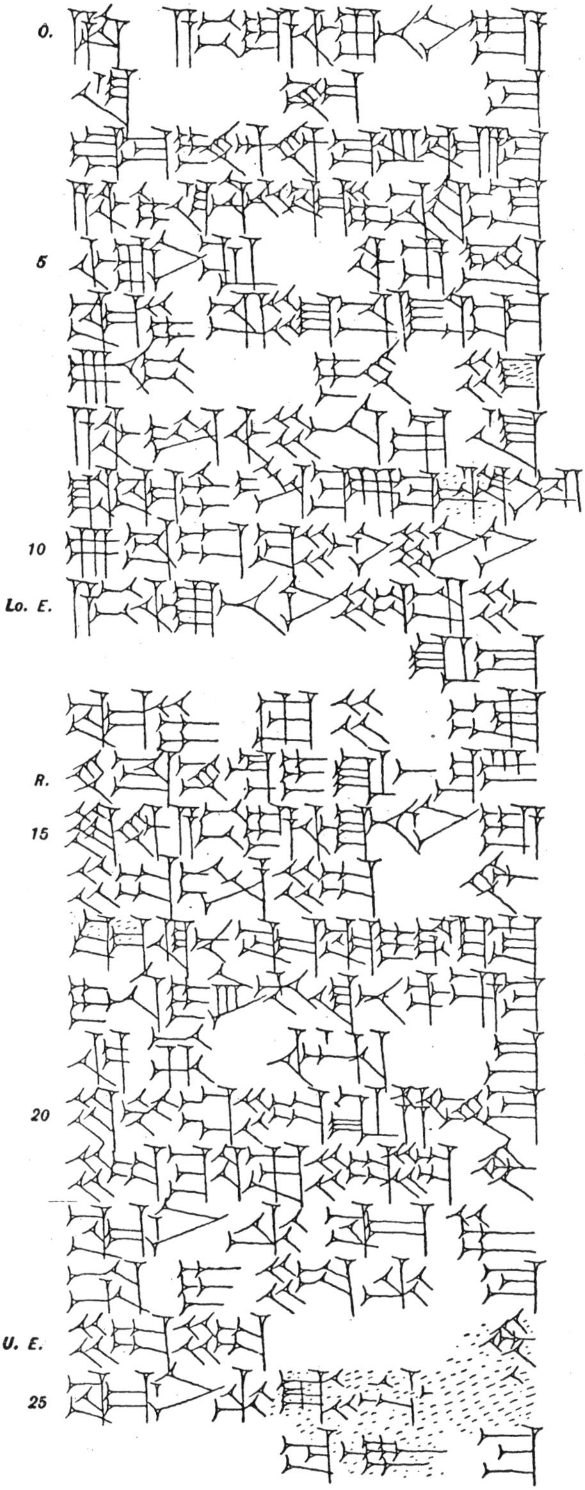

94

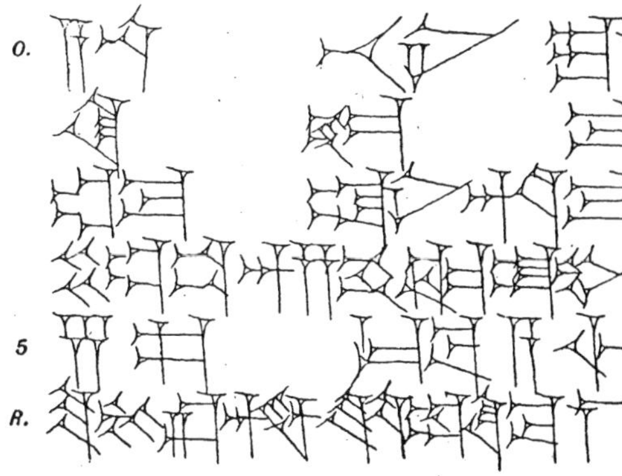

95

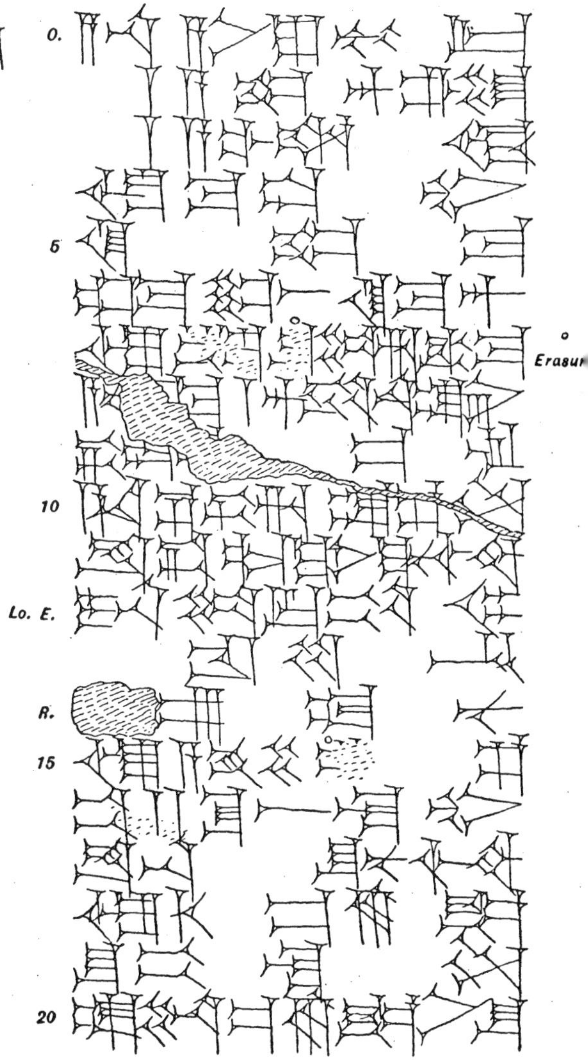

96

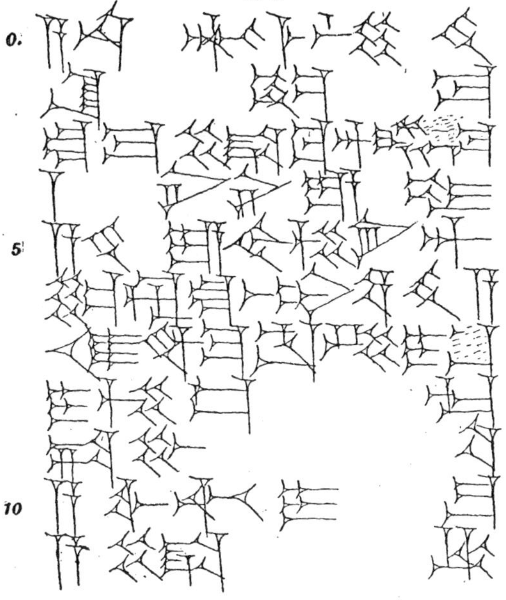

97

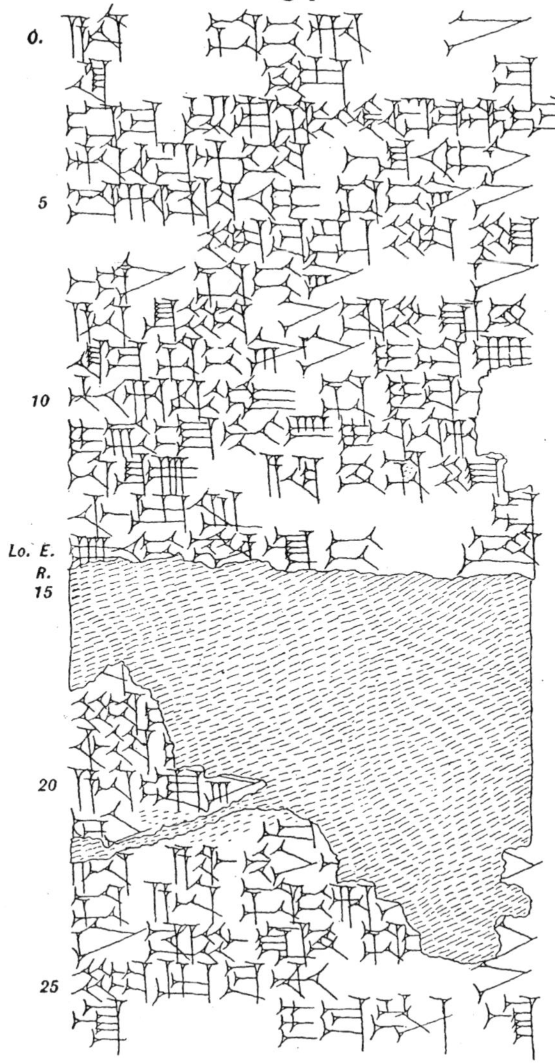

98

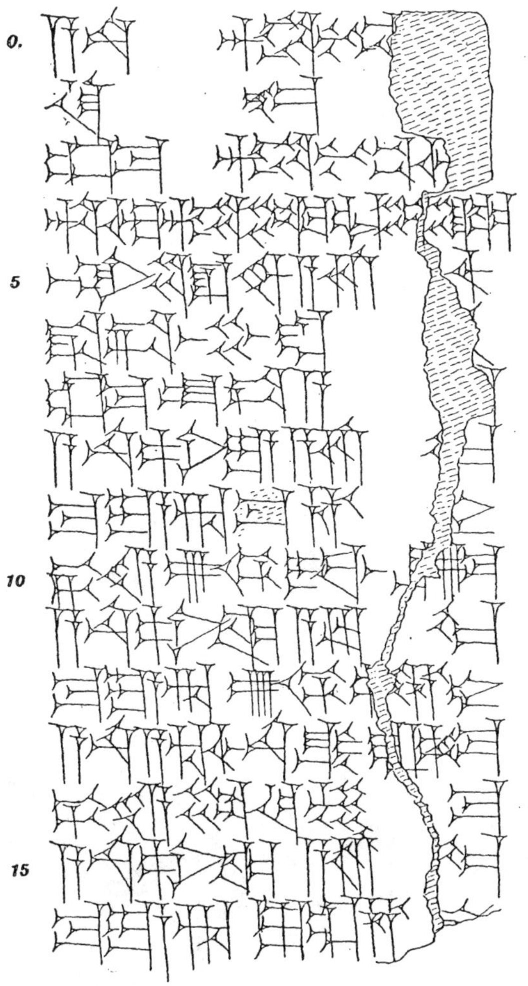

99

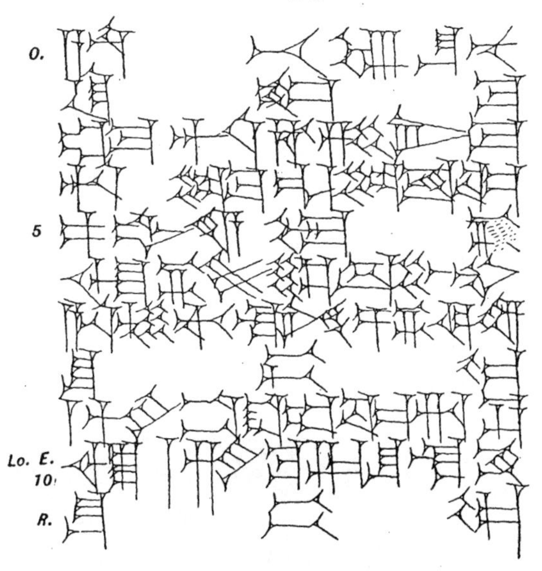

100

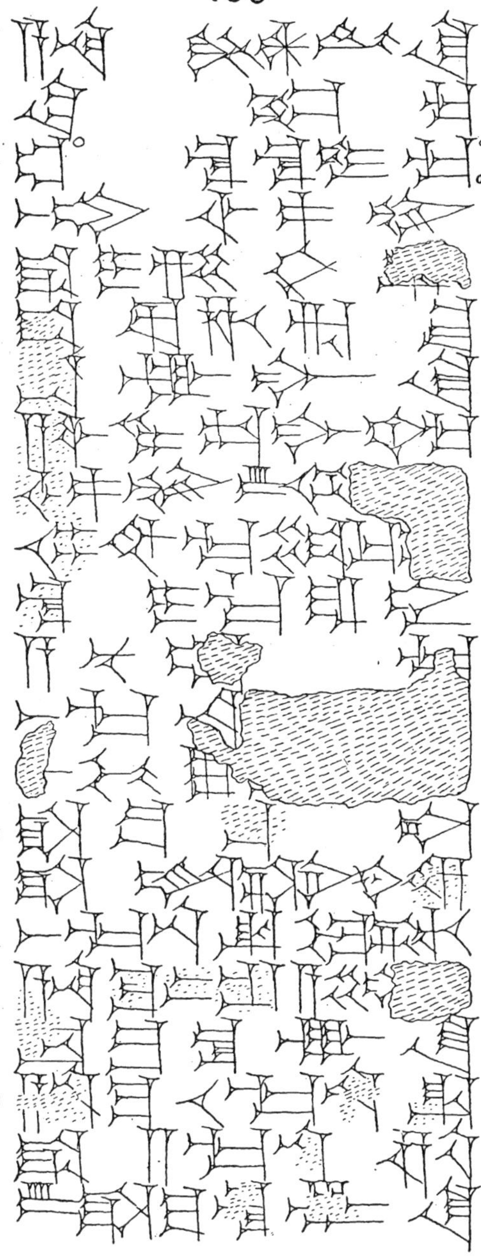
O.
omitted by scribe.
5
10
Lo. E.
R.
15
20

101

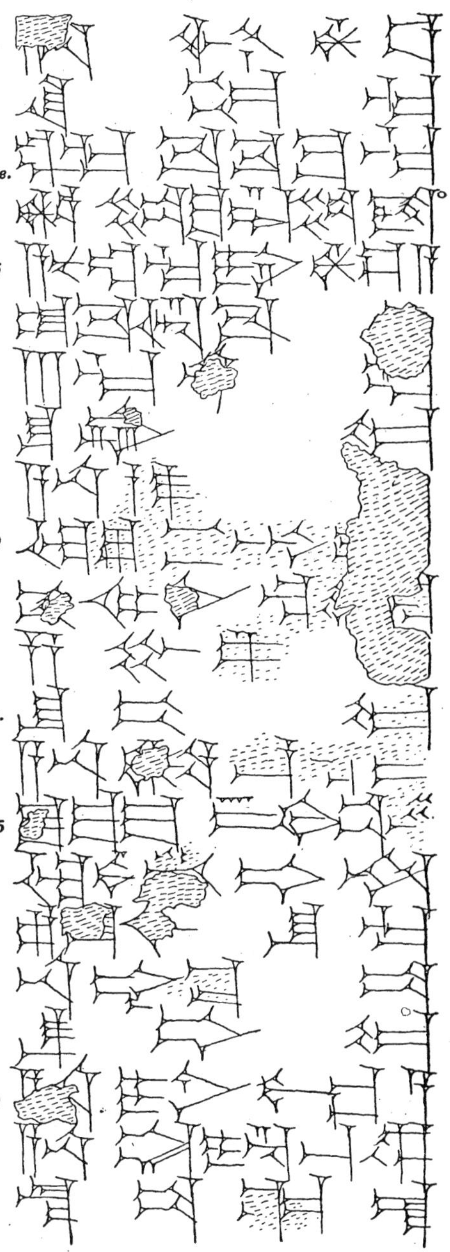
O.
5
10
R.
15
20

102

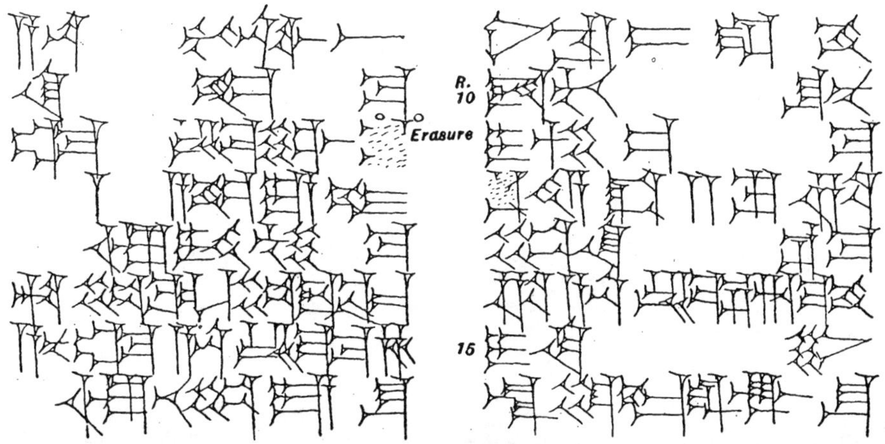
O.
Erasure
5
R.
10
15

103

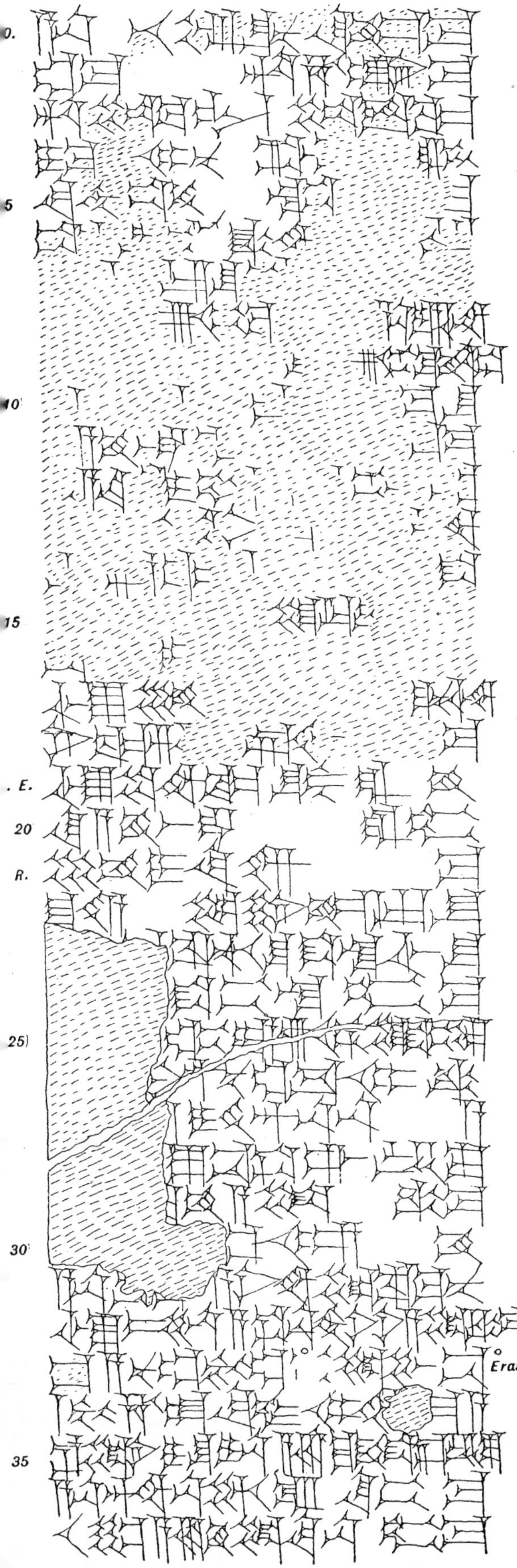

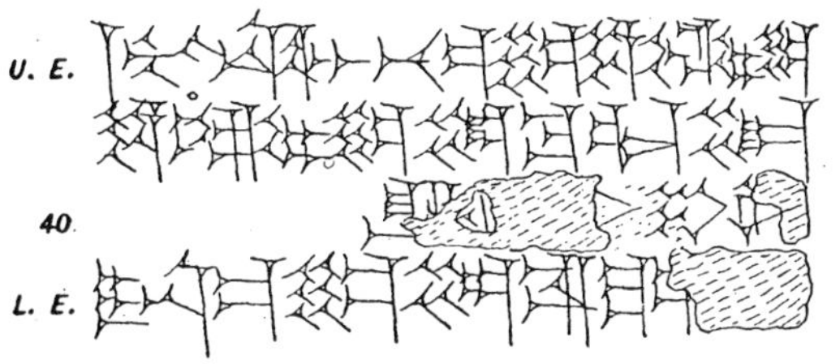

104

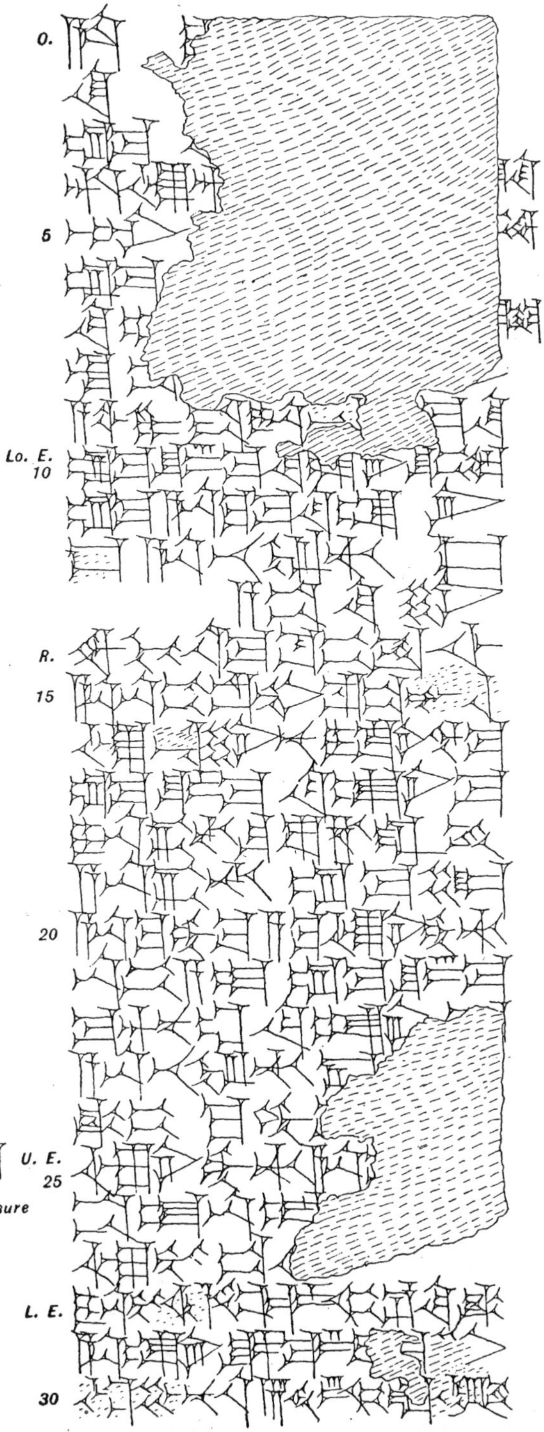

105

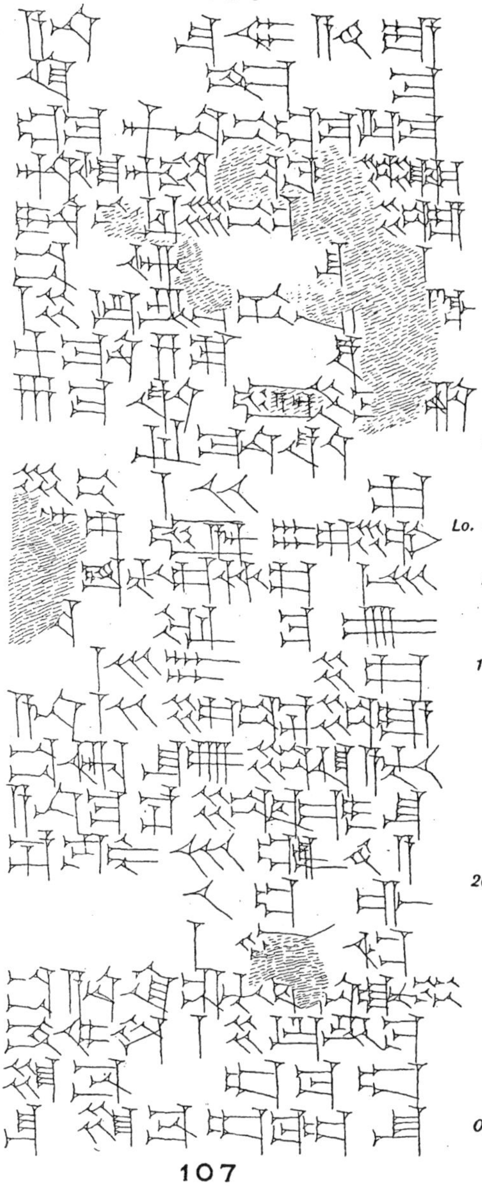

106

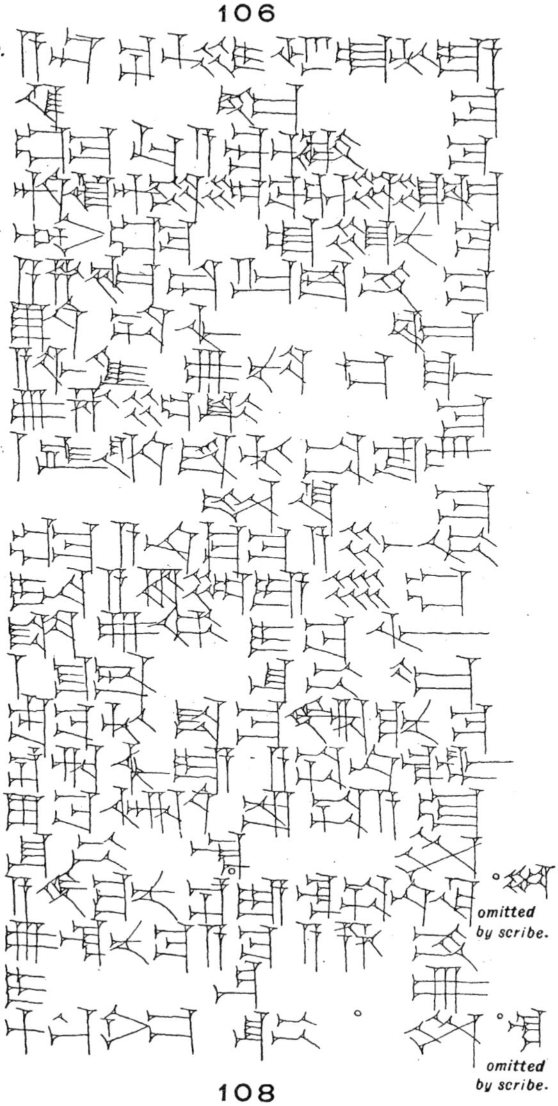

107

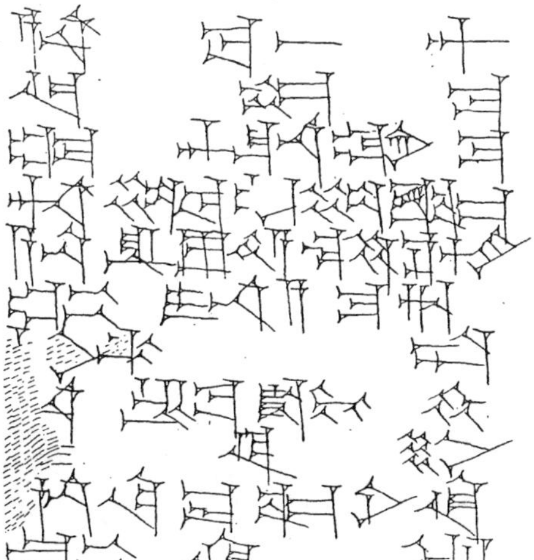

108

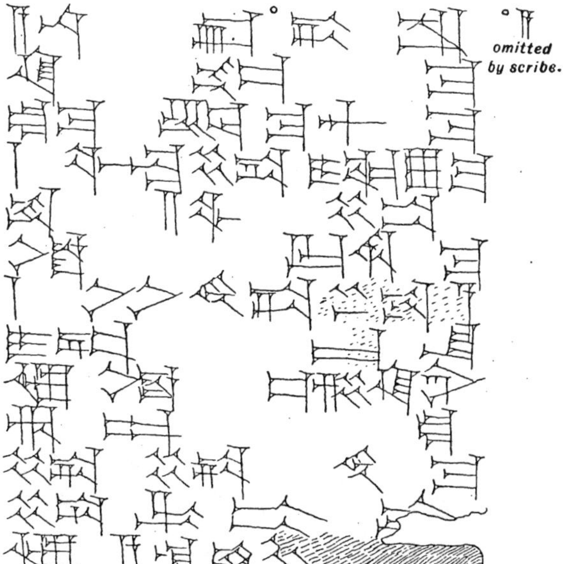

109

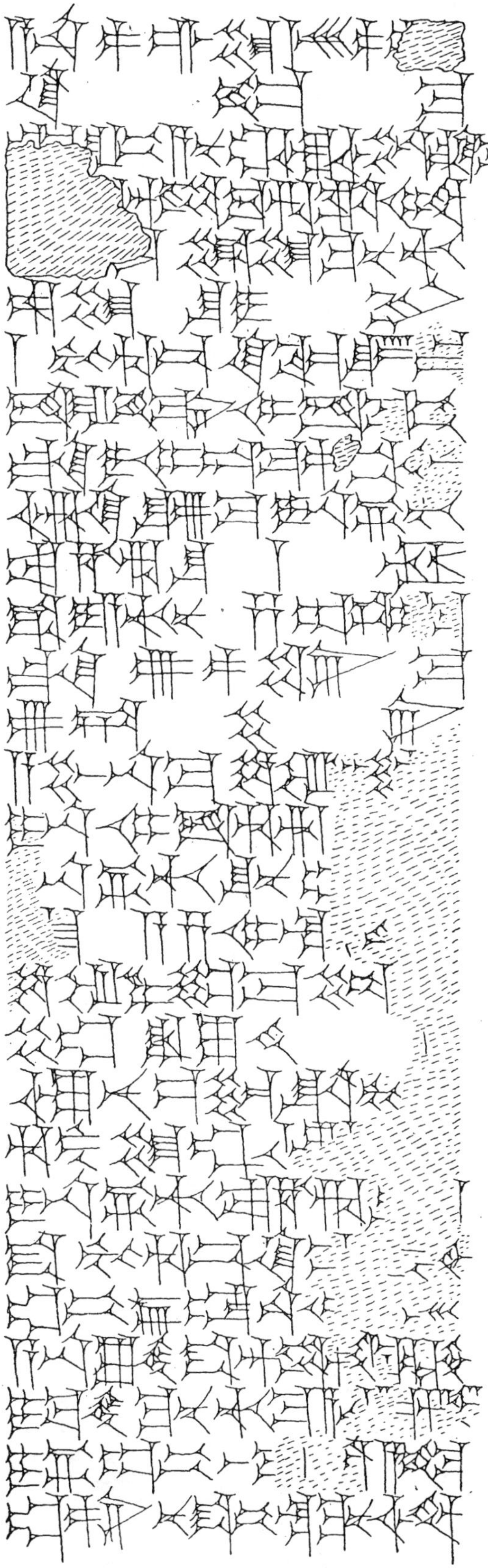

110

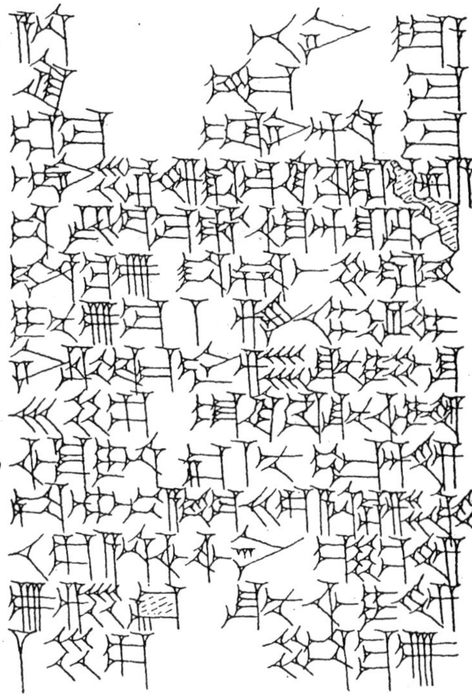

111

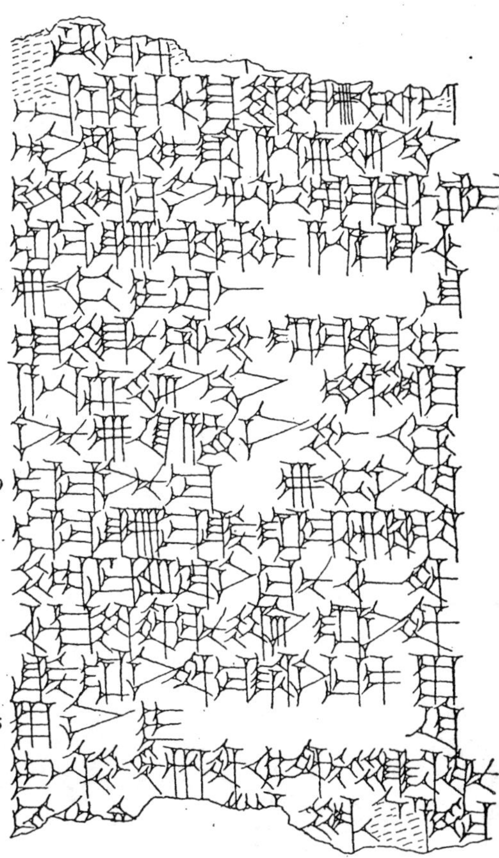

112

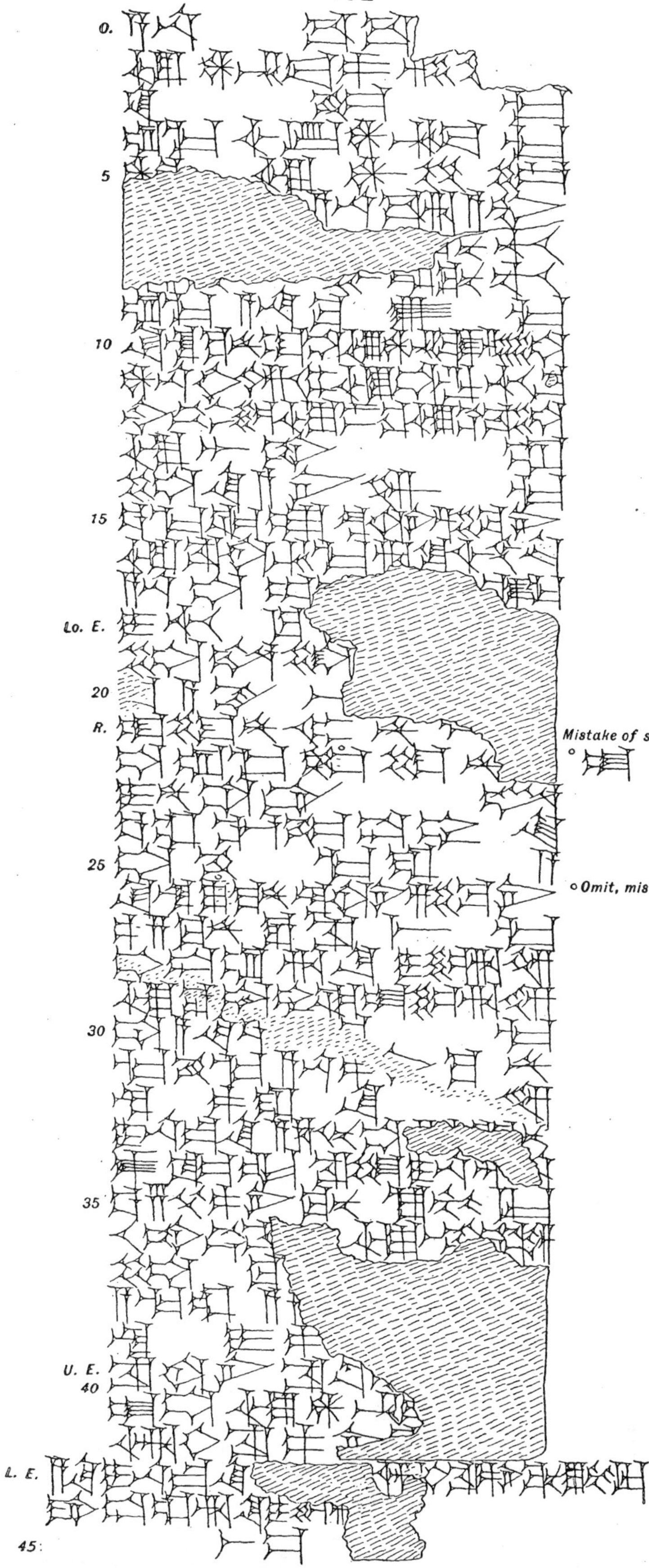

Mistake of scribe for

∘Omit, mistake of scribe.

113

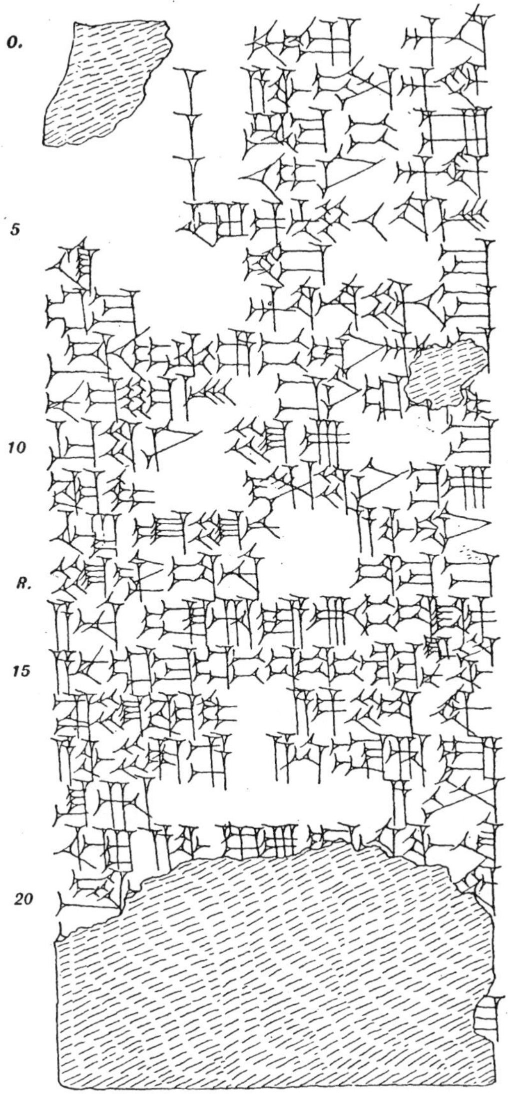

114

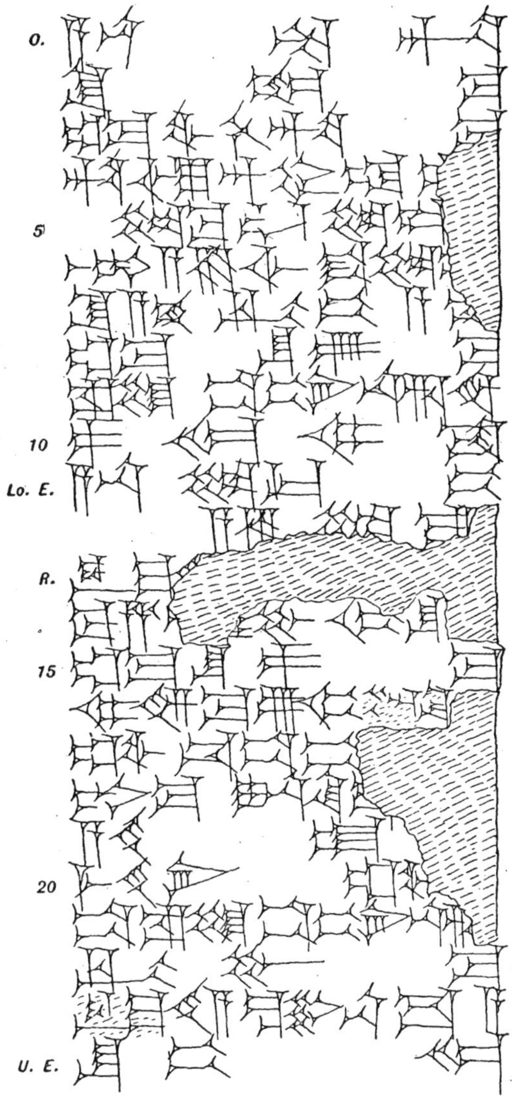

115

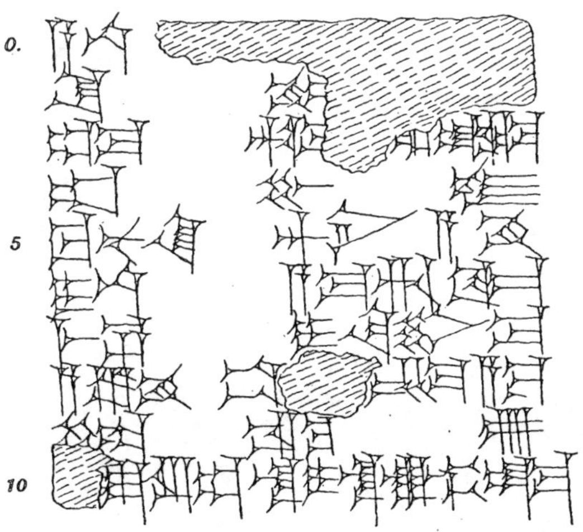

116

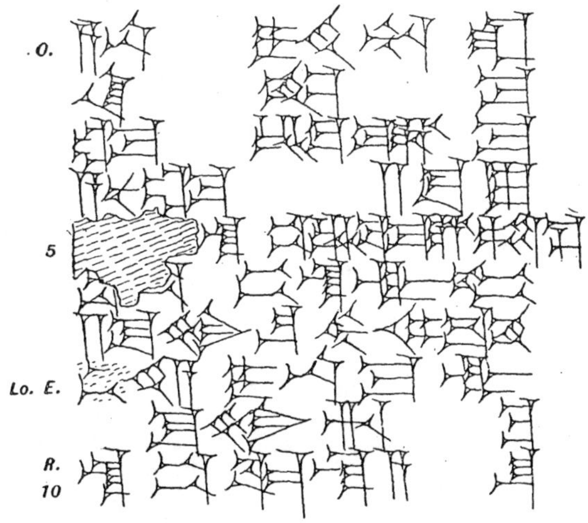

117

O.

Lo. E.

R.

U. E.

L. E.

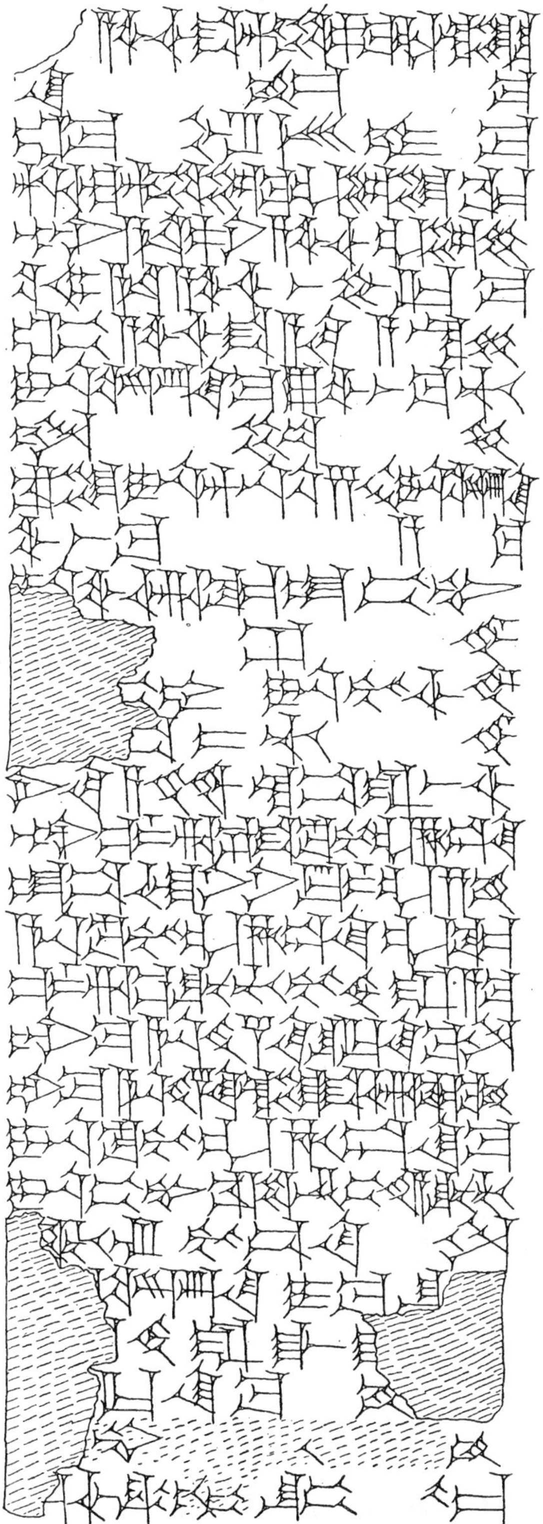

118

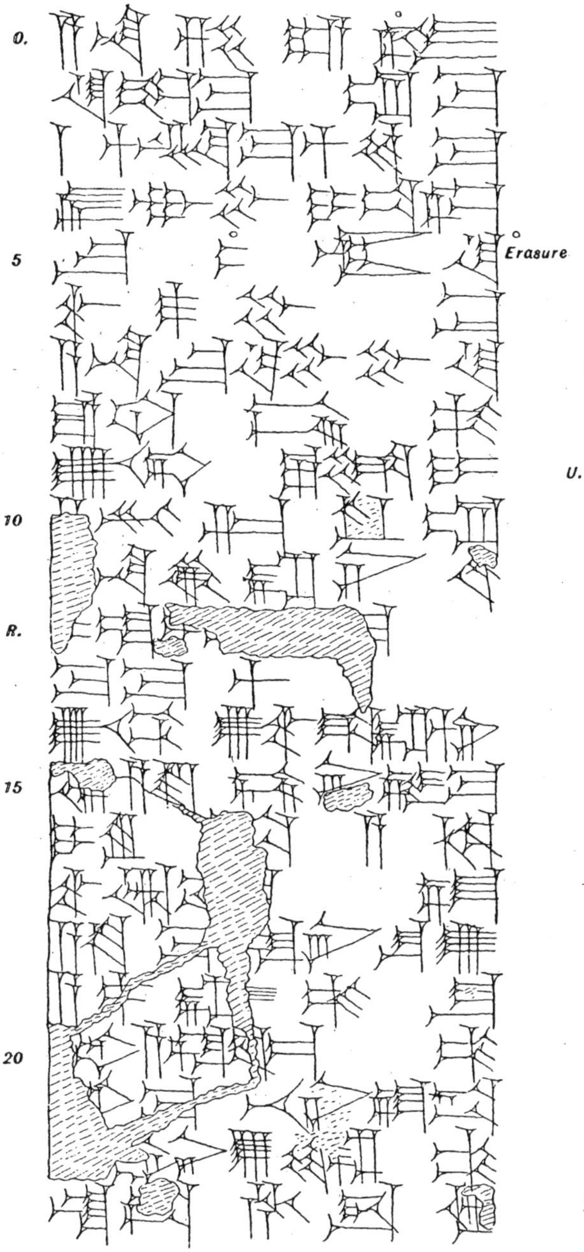

119

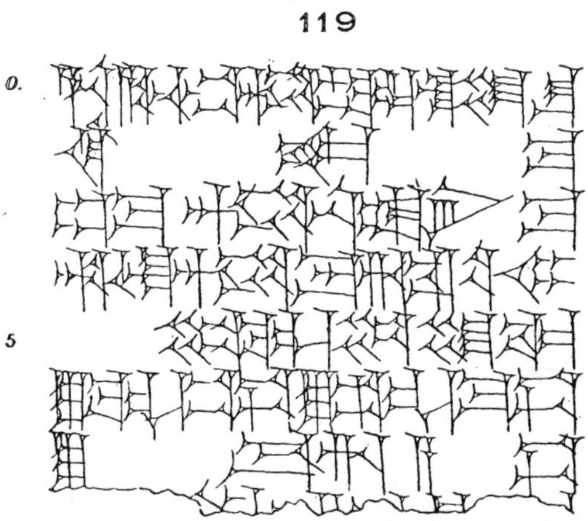

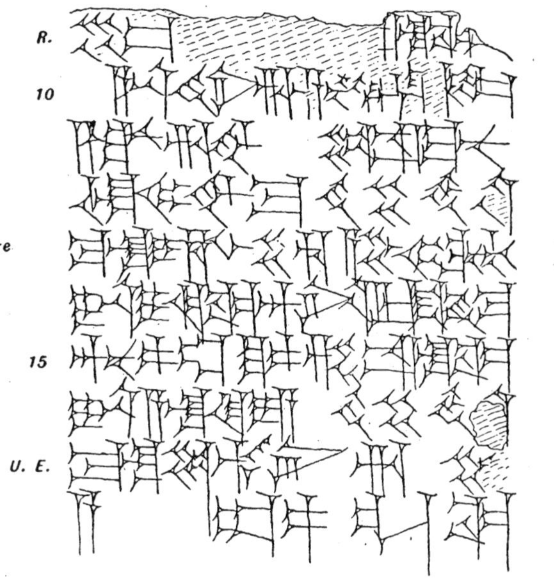

120

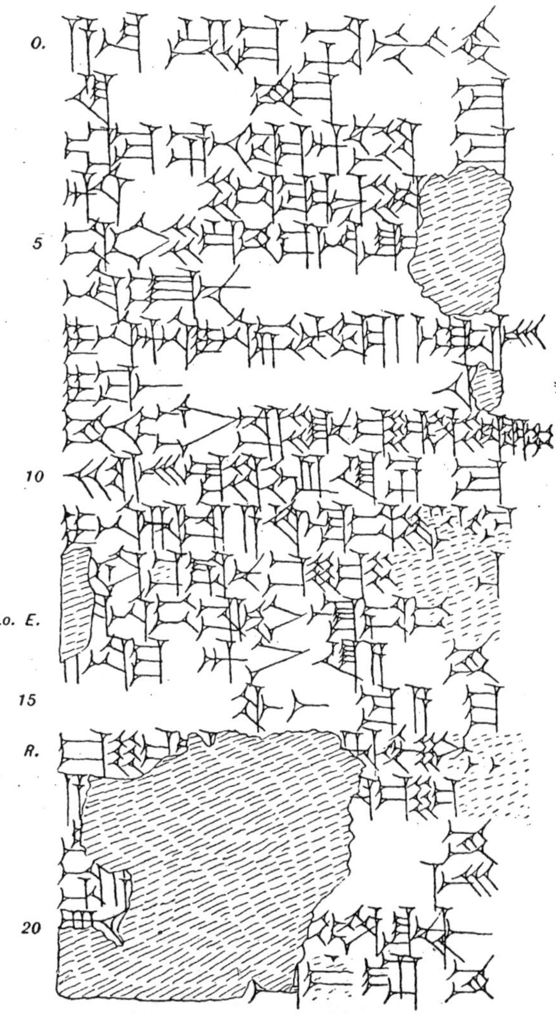

121

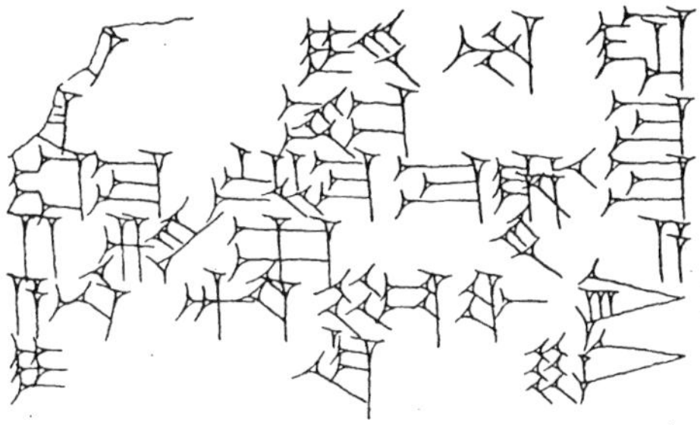

122

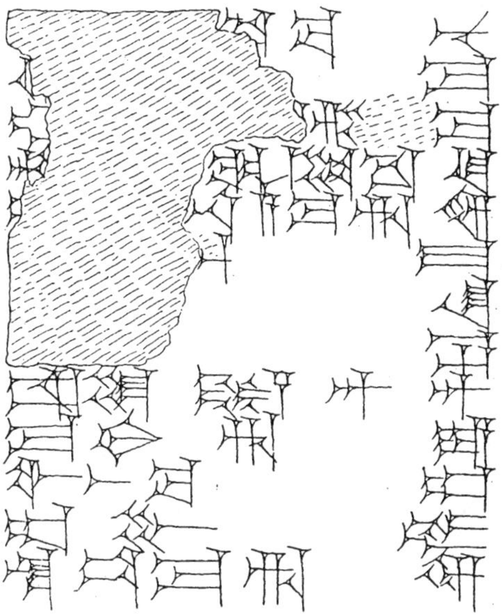

123

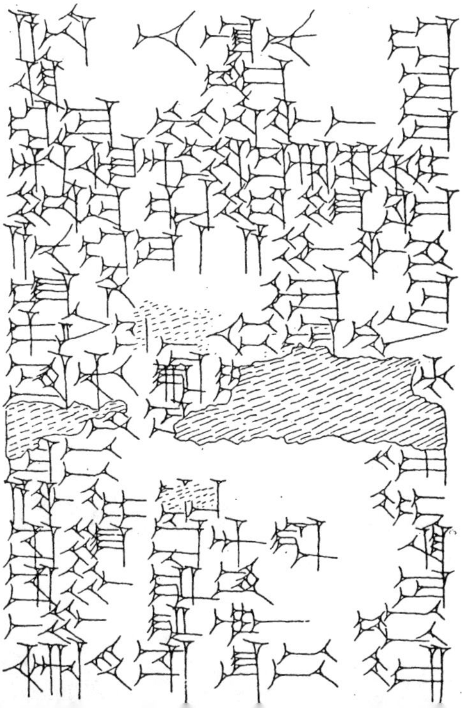

124

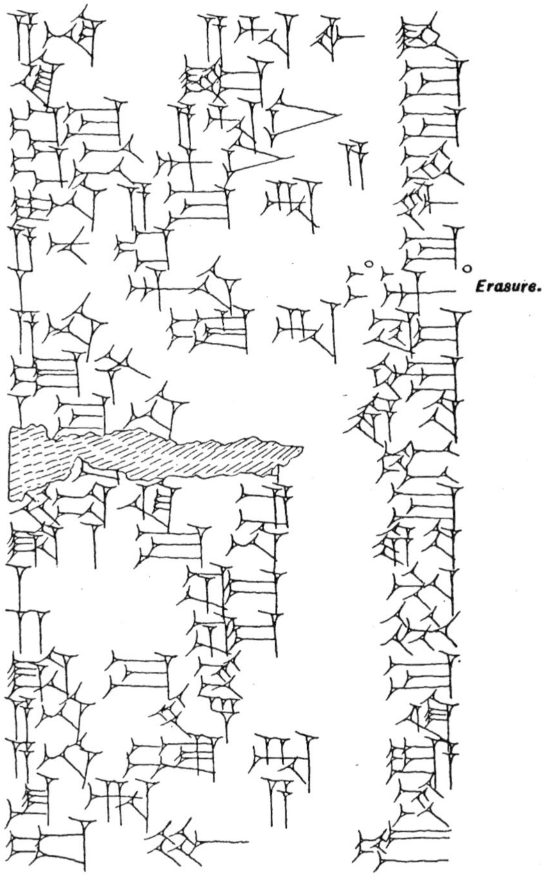

125

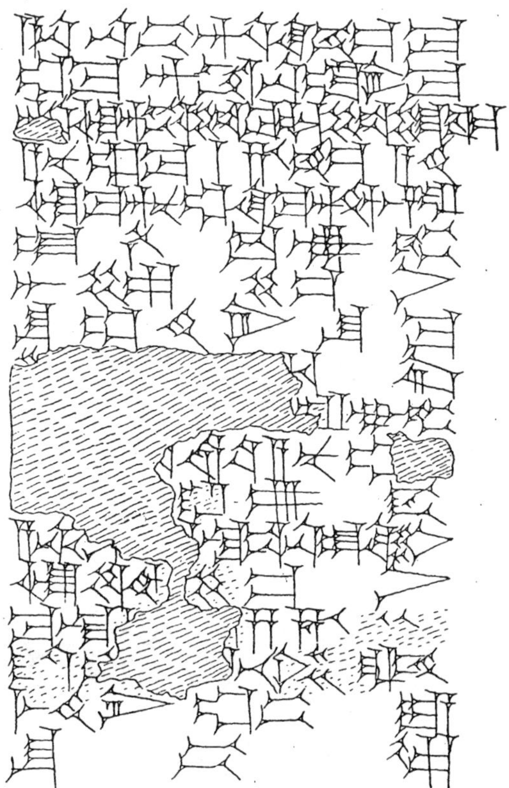

126

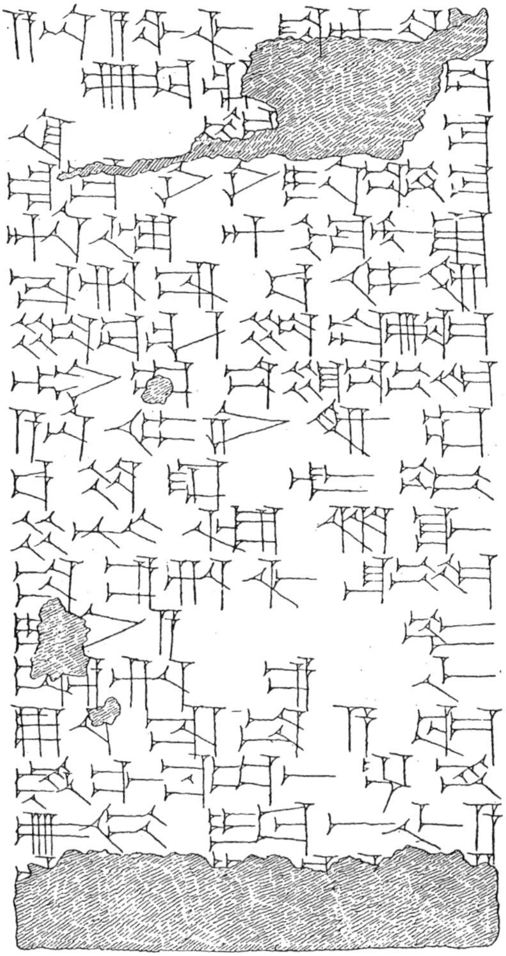

127

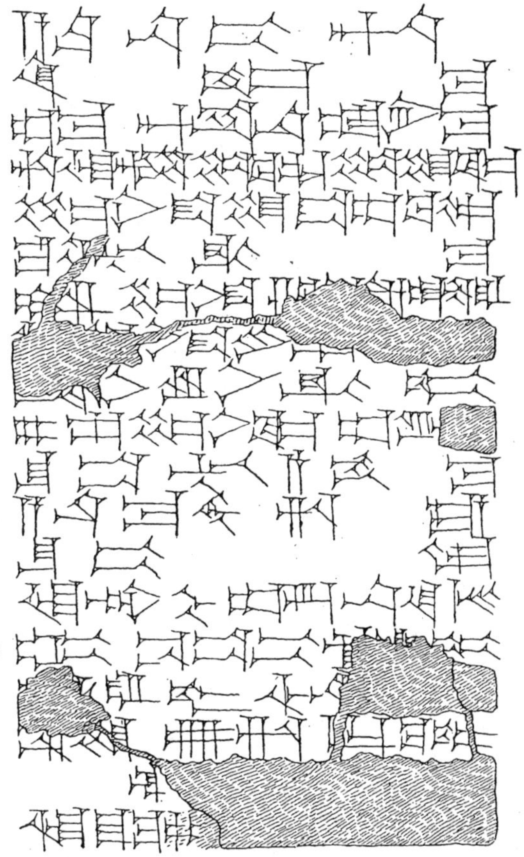

128

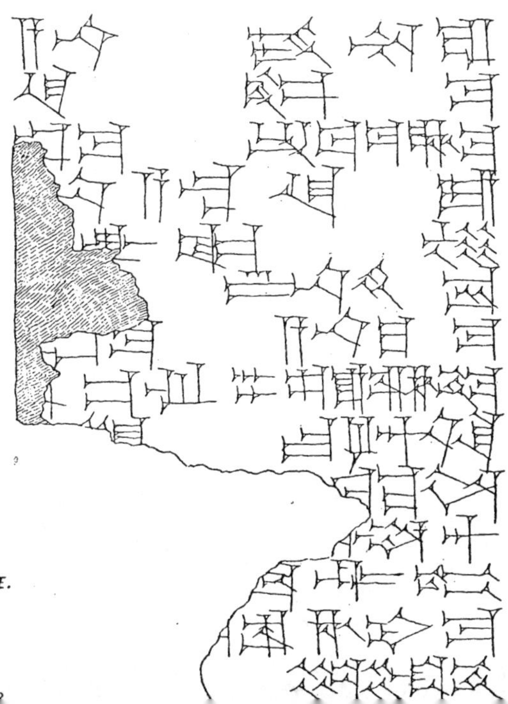

129

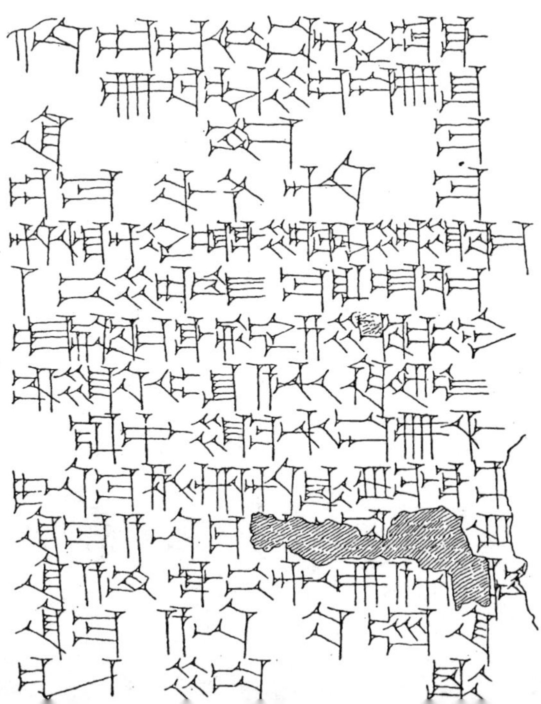

130

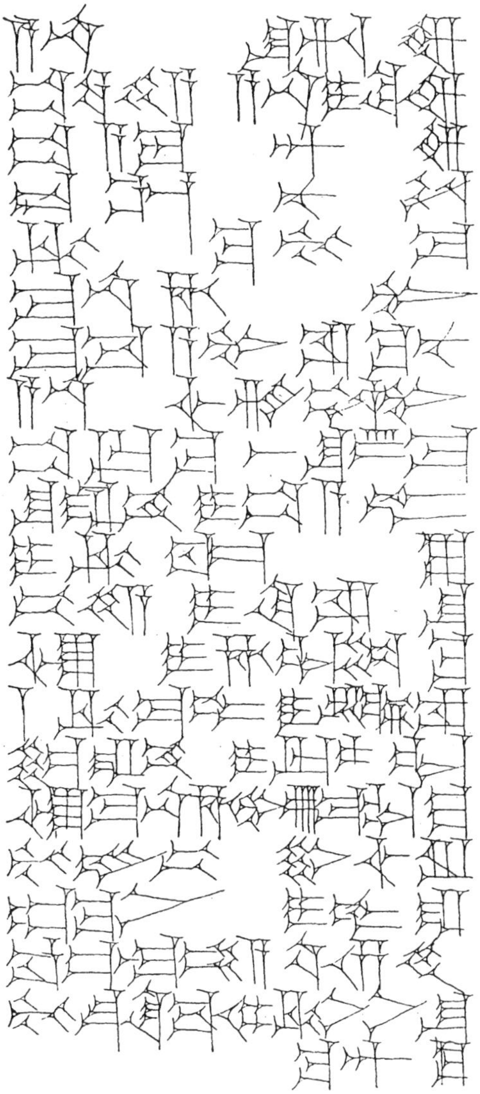

131

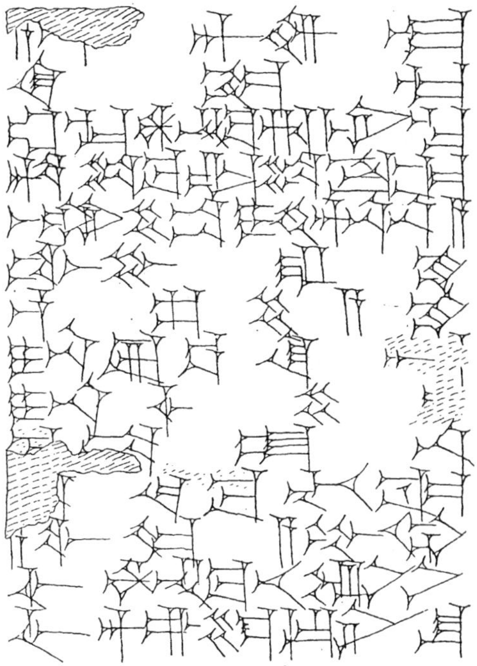

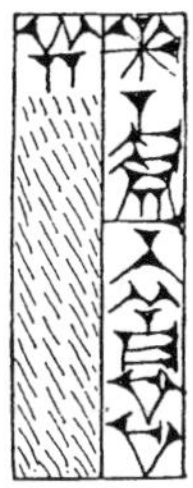

132

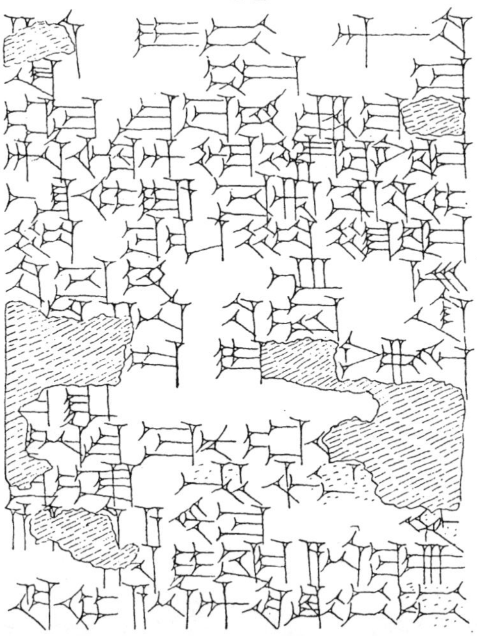

133

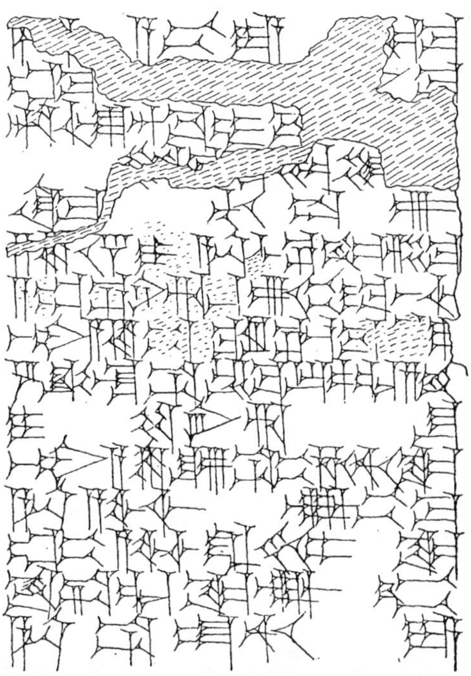

134

O.

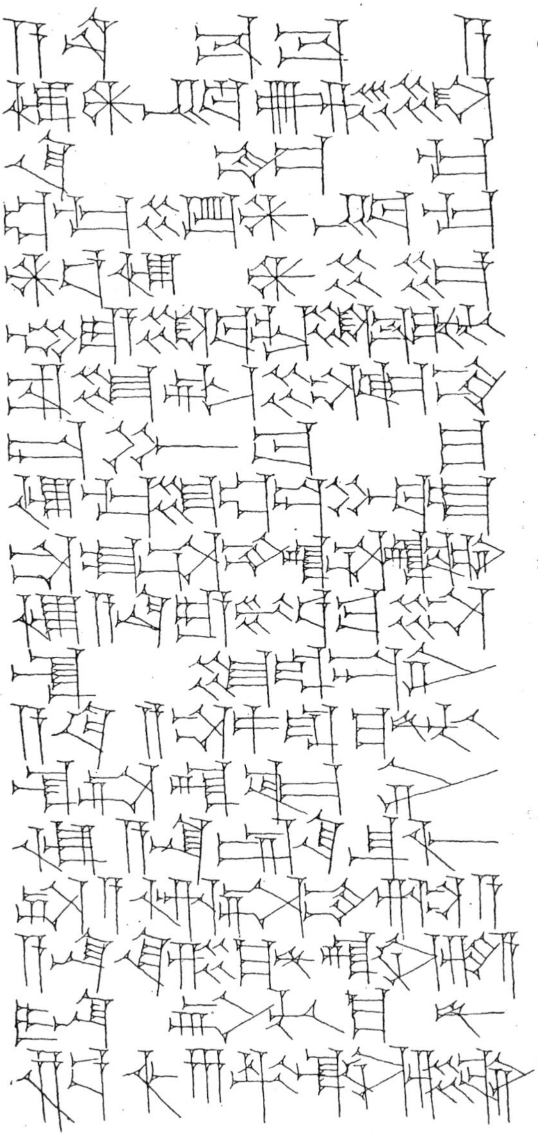

R.

135

O.

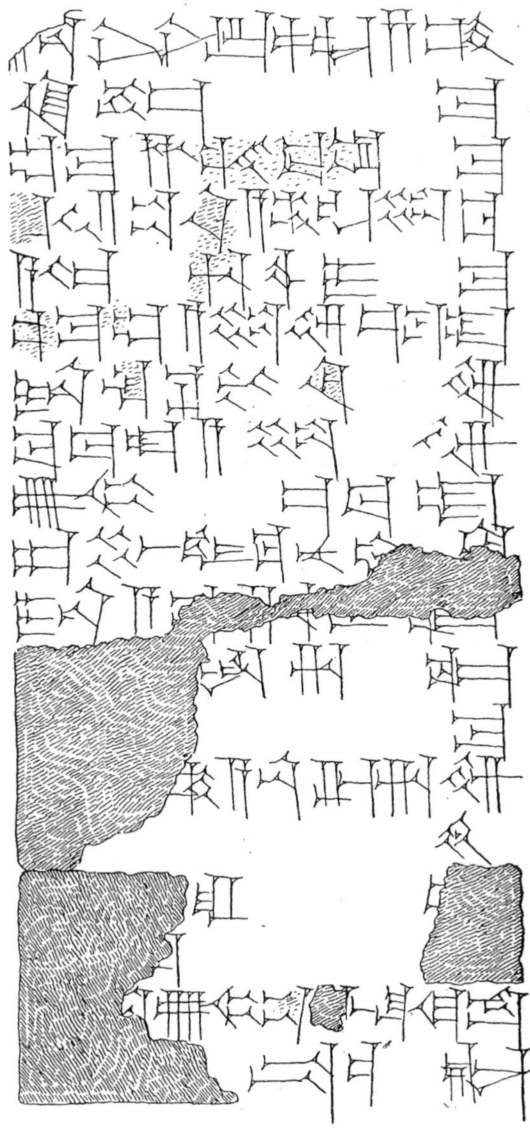

R.

136

O.

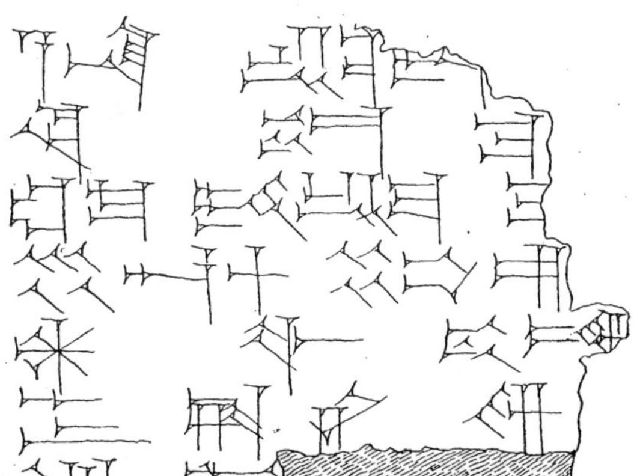

R.

137

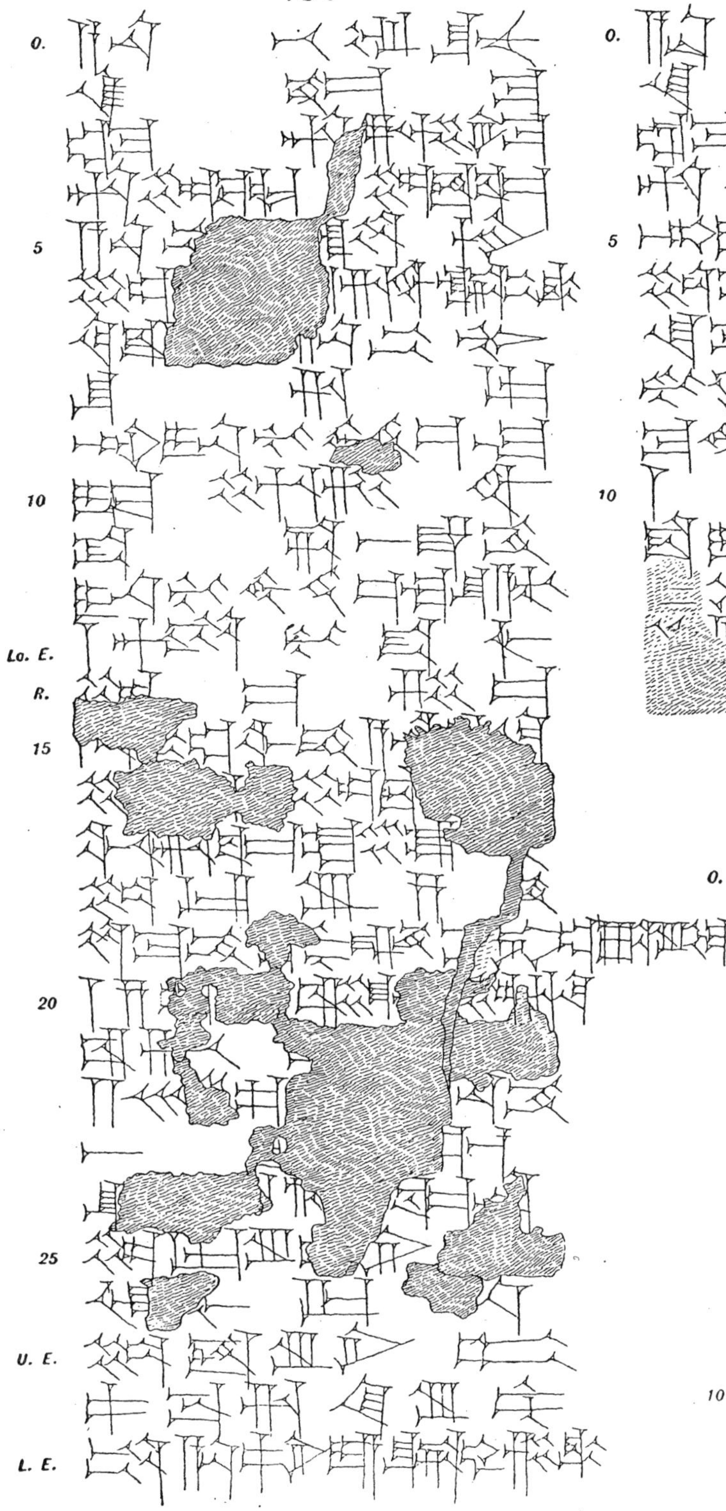

138

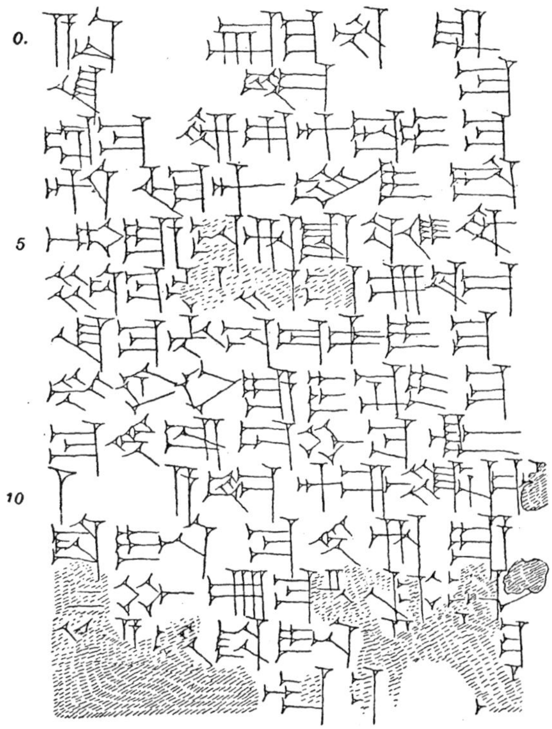

139

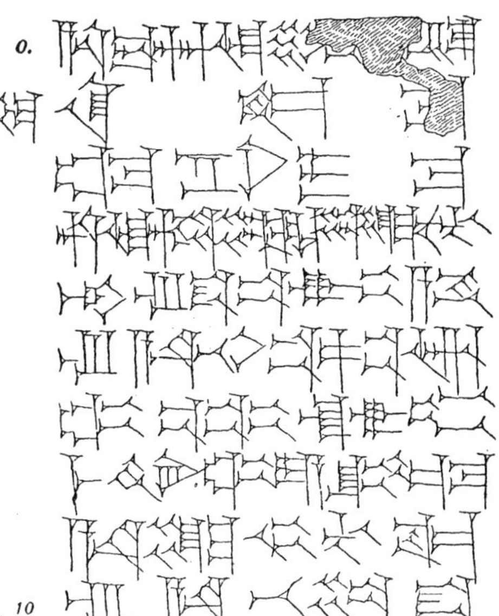

140

O. Lo. E. R.

141

O. Lo. E. R.

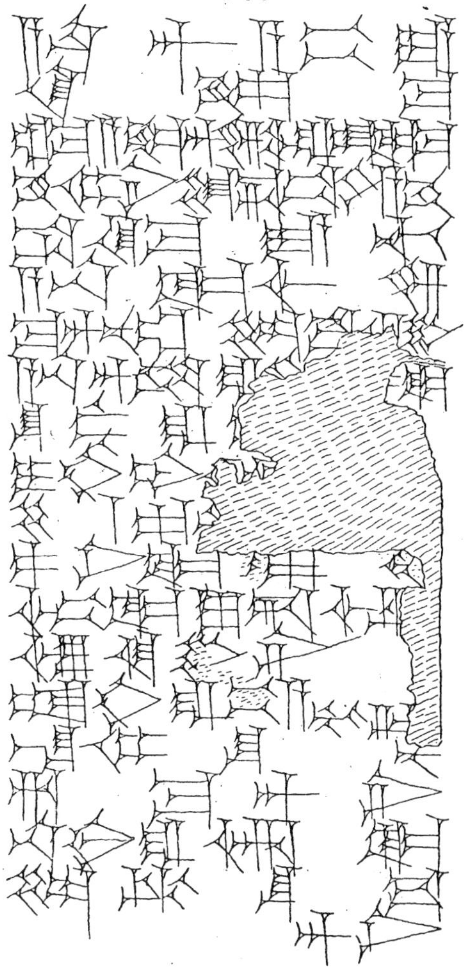

142

O. Lo. E. R.

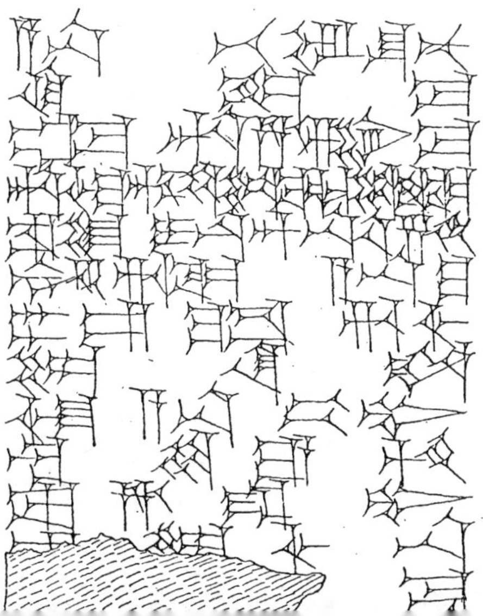

143

O. Lo. E. R.

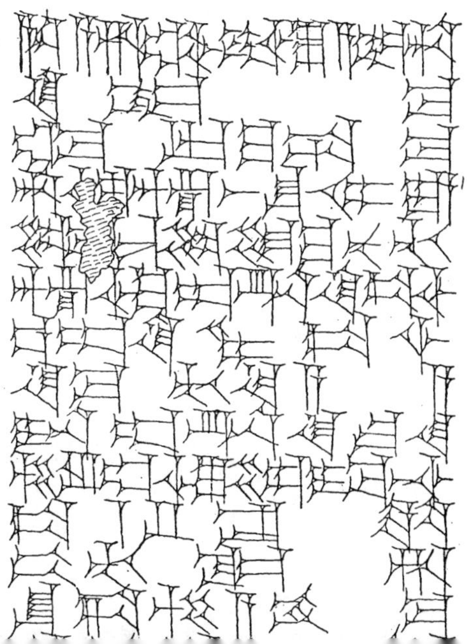

144

O.

Lo. E.

R.

U. E.

L. E.

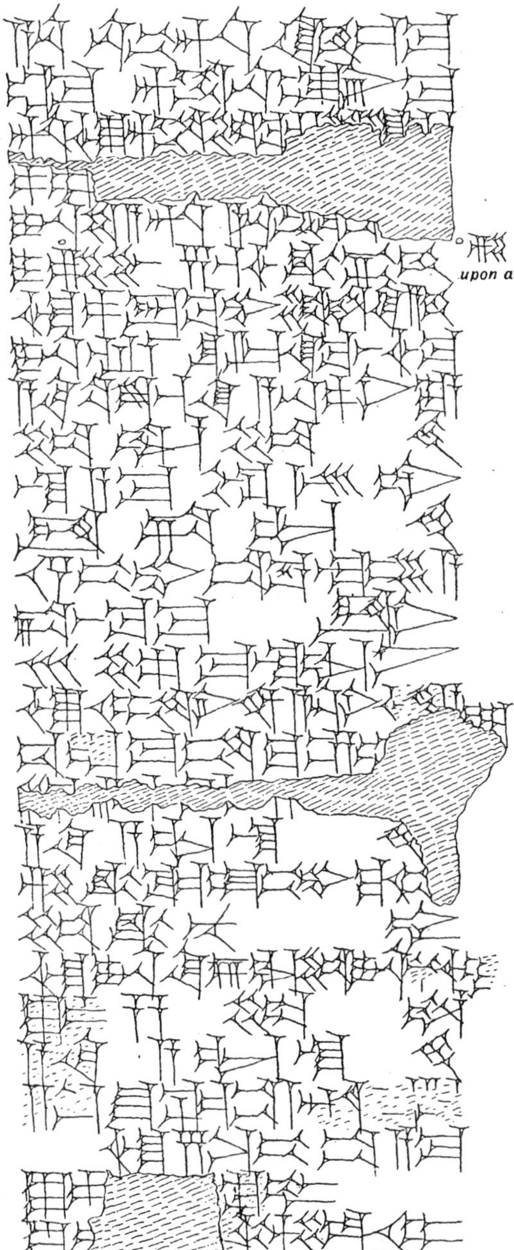

[sign] written upon an erasure.

145

O.

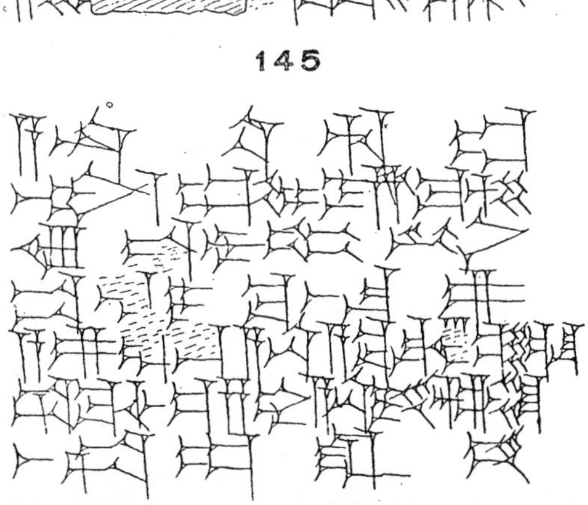

R.

U. E.

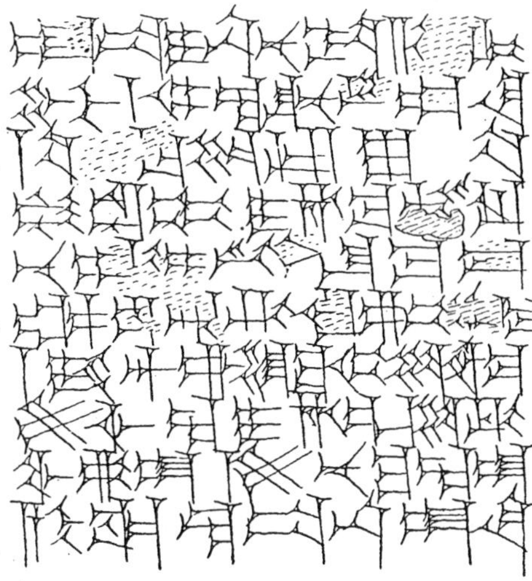

146

O.

R.

U. E.

L. E.

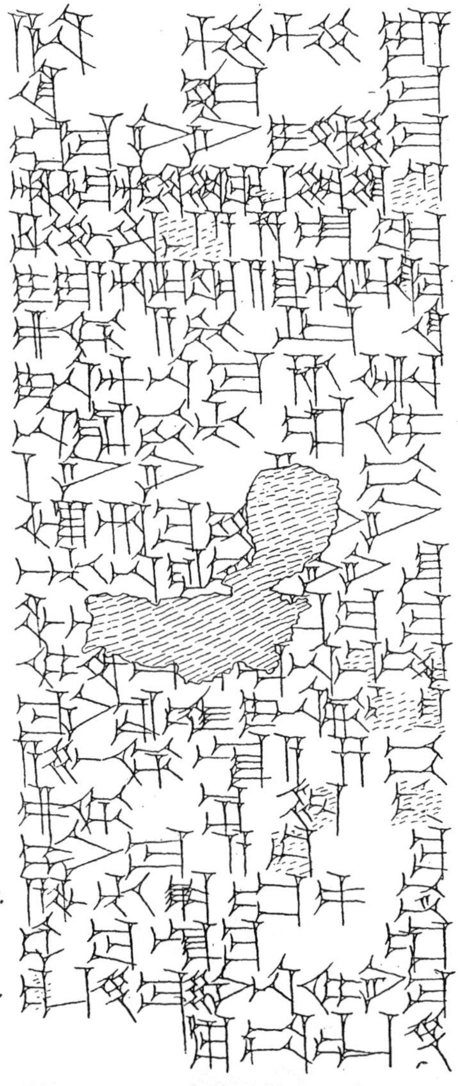

147

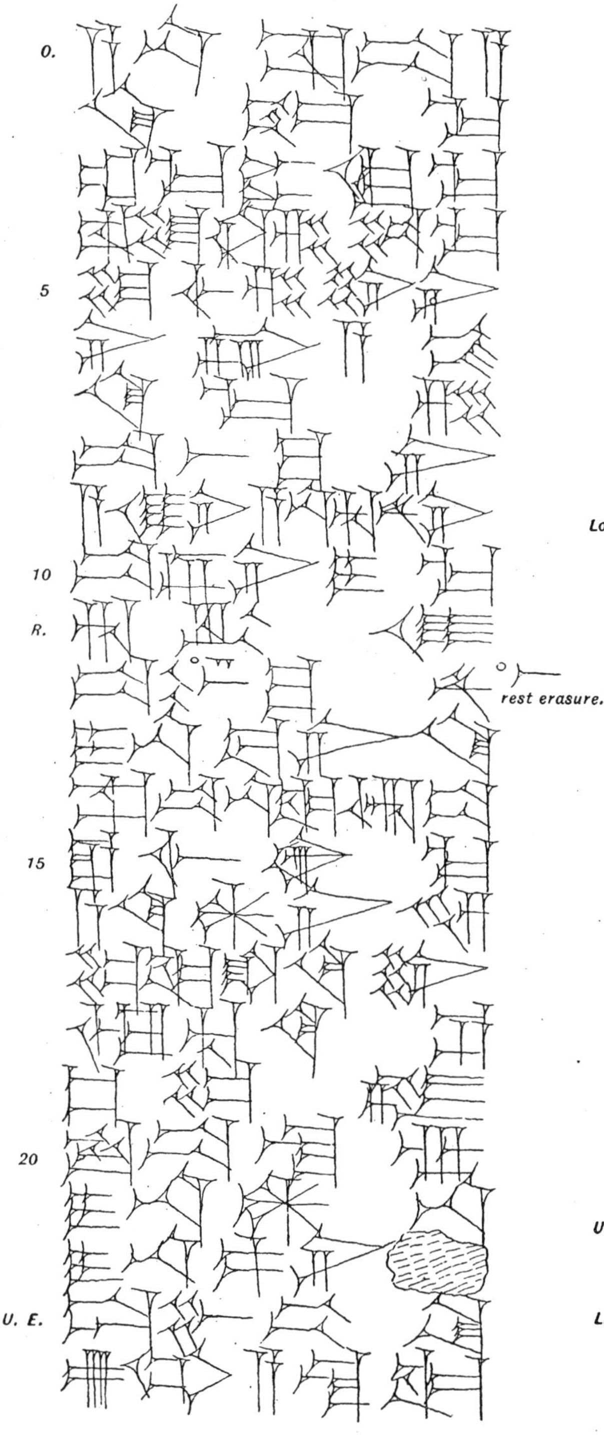

148

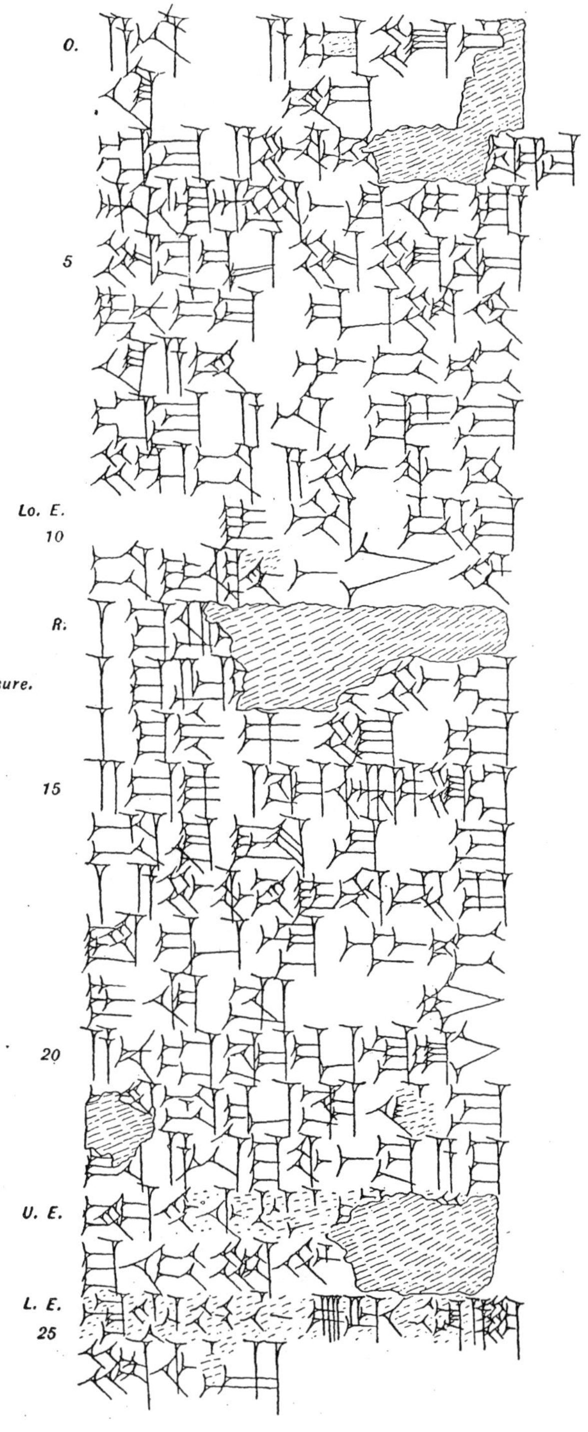

149

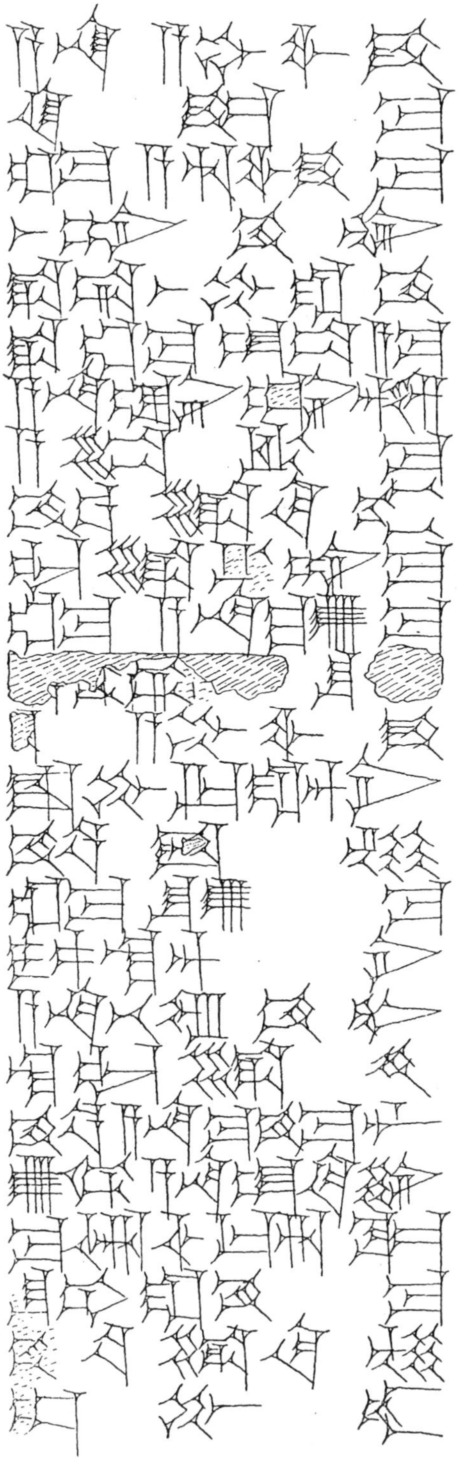

150

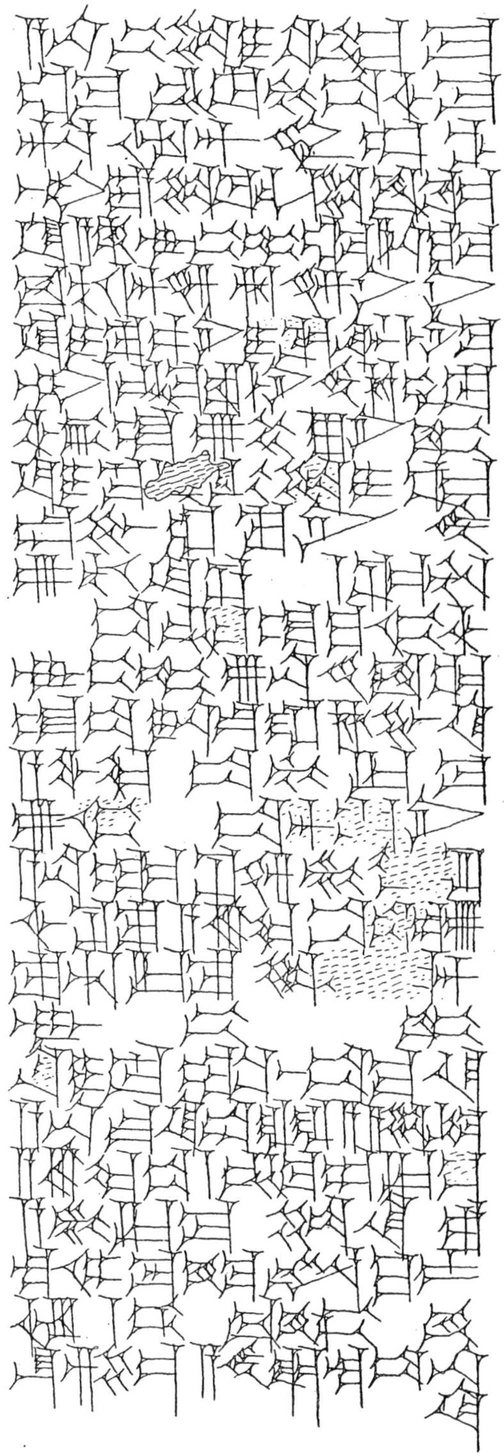

151

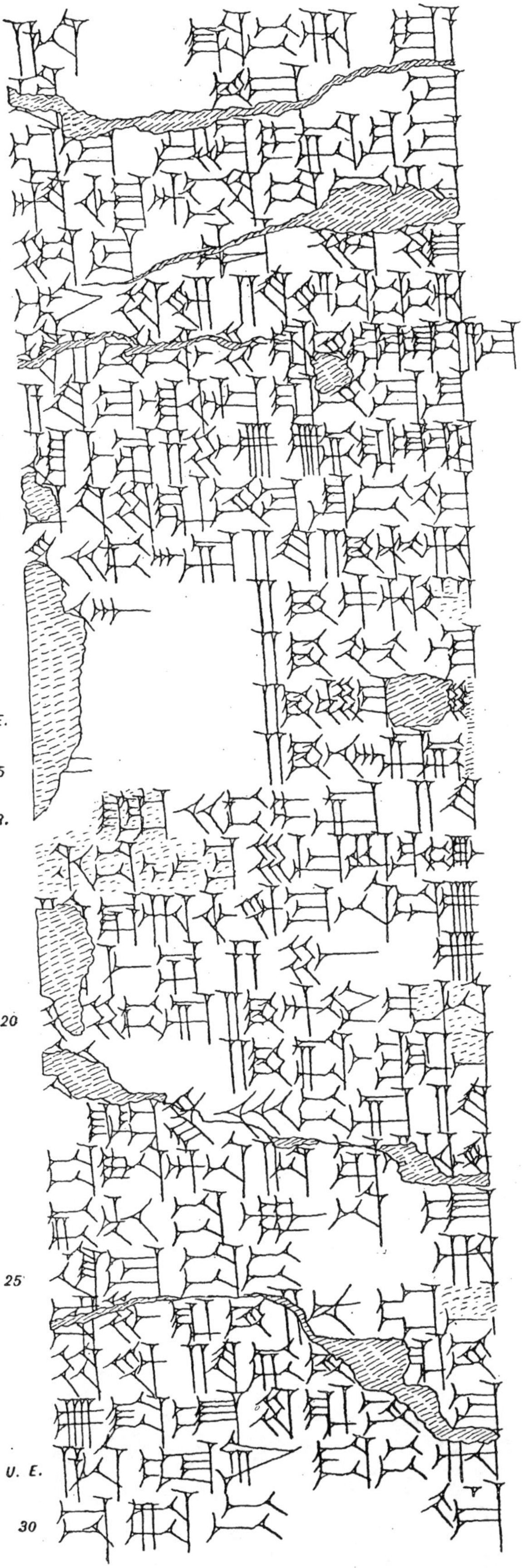

152

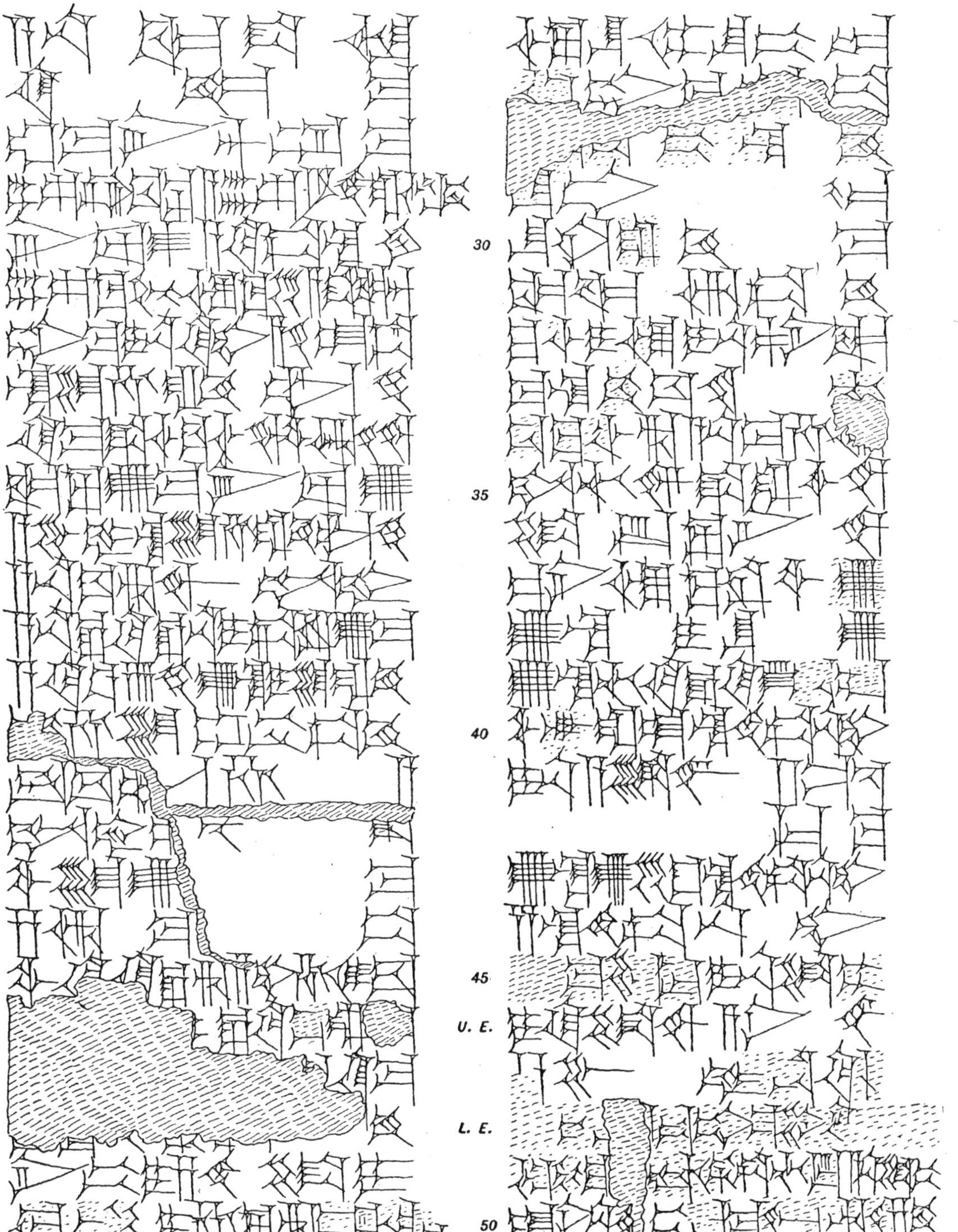

Lo. E.
R.
U. E.
L. E.